Sustainability Soup:

Selections of the Environmental Studies Association of Canada

Edited by Shirley Thompson, Ryan Katz-Rosene and Chris Ling

ESAC·ACÉE

esac press

1

Environmental Studies Association of Canada Press (ESAC Press) is the publishing arm of the Environmental Studies Association of Canada. This book is available at no cost at www.ESAC.ca

ESAC Press
c/o Dean's Office, Faculty of
Environmental Studies,
University of Waterloo
Waterloo, Ontario,
N2L 3G1 Canada

Phone: (519) 888-4442
Toll-Free: 1-866-437-2587
Fax: (519) 746-0292

ISBN-13: 978-1514137031

Cover by Adam Gibbard

CONTENTS

3

ACKNOWLEDGEMENTS

The editors would like to acknowledge our colleagues who contributed the chapters to this edited volume. Without their dedication, this book would not have been possible. Also, we want to express our appreciation to the many colleagues who undertook the review work. Their commitment to the project and thoughtful reviews greatly contributed to the quality of the book. Last but not least, we acknowledge both the Board of the Environmental Studies Association of Canada and ESAC Press for supporting the publishing of this book.

CONTRIBUTORS

Gary Bowden teaches environmental sociology at the University of New Brunswick - Fredericton. His interests include processes of long term stability and change in socio-ecological systems, the peak oil debate, and factors influencing the supply of, requirements for and adoption of social ingenuity.

Chris Buse is a doctoral candidate with the Dalla Lana School of Public Health, University of Toronto, a Research Associate with the Comparative Program on Health and Society, and a Doctoral Fellow with the CIHR Strategic Training Program in Public Health Policy.

Rebecca Hasdell is a doctoral candidate with the Dalla Lana School of Public Health, University of Toronto. She also holds a CIHR Frederick Banting and Charles Best Canada Graduate Scholarship Doctoral Award.

Maggie Ibrahim is working with World Vision UK as a resilience manager to ensure that programming and policy are risk informed. She has worked in sustainable livelihoods for the past 13 years, with the addition of disaster risk reduction and climate change adaptation expertise. She has worked through the Institute of Development Studies and non-government organisations such as Practical Action and Enda Tiers Monde. She is also passionate about governance, accountability and communications for social change. Most recently, Maggie has been concentrating on influencing the Post 2015 development agendas to ensure that they reflect the needs, wants and capacities of most marginalised groups.

Ryan Katz-Rosene is a SSHRC Post-Doctoral Fellow at the University of Ottawa's School of Political Studies, and sits on the Board of Directors of the Environmental Studies Association of Canada. He lives on a farm in Cantley, Québec.

Chris Ling is is the director of the School of Environment and Sustainability at Royal Roads University. He teaches sustainable development and is co-program head for the MA/MSc in Environmental

Management program. His main areas of research concern urban, post-industrial and multi-functional landscapes and sustainable community development. He was also the Co-president of the Environmental Studies Association of Canada from 2010-2014.

David McRobert is an environmental, energy and aboriginal rights lawyer working out of offices in Toronto and Peterborough, Ontario. Between 1990 and 2011 he was a part-time Professor teaching environmental and business law courses at York University, University of Toronto and Humber College.

Lenore Newman's love affair with food began on her family's fishing boats. She holds a Canada Research Chair in Food Security and Environment at the University of the Fraser Valley, where she runs a research program focused on Canadian regional cuisines, local food sovereignty, culturally preferred foods, and urban food systems.

H. Carolyn Peach Brown is an Assistant Professor and Director of Environmental Studies at the University of Prince Edward Island, Canada. Prior to doing her PhD in Natural Resource Policy and Management at Cornell University, she worked for over 10 years in Central Africa at the grass roots level in community development. Carolyn's research focuses on environmental governance for management of commons resources, and how such strategies can contribute to the goals of sustainable resource management and improved livelihoods. In particular, she explores the role played by communities and civil society groups in multi-level governance, in the context of changing policy and a changing climate.

Cheryl Teelucksingh is an Associate Professor at Ryerson University in the Sociology Department and a member of the Yeates School of Graduate Studies at Ryerson University Ryerson University. Dr. Teelucksingh is also principal investigator for SSHRC funded (2013-2016) grant "The Green Gap: Toward Inclusivity in Toronto's Green Employment".

Shirley Thompson is an associate professor at the Natural Resources Institute at the University of Manitoba. She researches sustainable livelihoods, food sovereignty and renewable energy with a focus on First Nation issues. She was the Co-president of the Environmental Studies Association of Canada from 2010-2014 with Chris Ling.

Nicola Ward has worked in international development for a number of organisations over the last 10 years, and been specialising in climate change adaptation and risk reduction for the last five. She is currently working with CARE International as the Learning and Evidence Specialist for the Adaptation Learning Programme for Africa (ALP) which aims to increase the capacity of vulnerable households in sub-Saharan Africa to adapt to climate variability and change through community-based adaptation approaches.

INTRODUCTION

Dr. Shirley Thompson
Associate Professor
Natural Resources Institute, University of Manitoba

Dr. Ryan Katz-Rosene
SSHRC Post-Doctoral Fellow
School of Political Studies, University of Ottawa

Dr. Chris Ling
Director, School of Environment and Sustainability
Royal Roads University

Each year members of the Environmental Studies Association of Canada (ESAC) convene at the organization's Annual Conference to network, share their research, and debate ideas regarding sustainability and the future of the planet. In part this book is the outgrowth of such research and subsequent discussions following the Annual Conferences held in 2013 and 2014, held at the University of Victoria and Brock University, respectively. Participants at those conferences and the broader ESAC community were invited to submit work for inclusion in a book on the theme of sustainability. All manuscripts went through a blind review process. The result is a medley – a 'sustainability soup' if you will – of proscriptive, critical and insightful analyses into the current and future prospects for a sustainable planet.

The chapters herein cross a number of themes tacitly confronting a distinct dimension of climate change. While the scientific community has increasingly built a consensus on the role of human activity in contributing to climatic change, the question of *how we respond* – as individuals, as communities, as nations, and as a species – is evermore on the minds of social scientists and in particular scholars of environmental studies. The chapters in this book each confront a distinct component of our collective response to climate change, and in doing so each provides an ingredient in the vast recipe for Earth's sustainability soup!

In the first chapter, Lenore Newman considers the potential disruption of the production of three iconic Canadian foods; ice wine, maple syrup, and salmon. Newman considers how climate change might compromise Canada's social and cultural food security. The impact of climate change on Canadian cuisine is considered within the context of concepts of the outdoors, winter, and wilderness.

In the second chapter, Carolyn Peach Brown, Maggie Ibrahim and Nicole Ward outline how to build adaptive capacity through addressing unsustainable land management through Farmer-Managed Natural Regeneration (FMNR) on degraded land in Africa. This is discussed in the context of the broader literature on international development and climate change using the lens of the local adaptive capacity framework for two case studies, one in Ghana and the other in Ethiopia. Through this agroforestry approach, farmers were able to manage the naturally occurring regrowth of shoots from the stumps of trees that are present in their fields which has increased agricultural production and income levels of farmers. The introduction of FMNR has been successful in fostering improved adaptive capacity and resilience to climate change in communities in Ethiopia and Ghana.

In the third chapter, Chris Buse, Cheryl Teelucksingh and Rebecca Hasdell discuss how wind turbines (WTs) and other renewable sources of energy are increasingly being used to tackle energy insecurity and environmental concerns such as climate change. As alternative energy generation continues to become more palatable to decision-makers in North America, WTs have emerged as a controversial topic in environmental public health. This chapter offers an alternative framing to existing debates over the direct health effects of wind turbines. They employ a political economy perspective to emphasize the importance of questioning the power inequalities between stakeholders in order to draw attention to the often overlooked psychosocial pathways to ill-health, and the role of social and procedural justice as it relates to WT siting and

9

management. Drawing from in-depth interviews with Toronto's environmental NGO professionals, they discuss how community power has been received throughout the province and theorize that community power projects can offer an alternative discourse around WTs by changing the power dynamic of community *versus* wind developer, to community *as* wind developer.

In the fourth chapter, Gary Bowden discusses three major approaches to addressing the climate problem: mitigation, adaption and geoengineering. Geoengineering involves large-scale engineering of our environment in order to combat or counteract the effects of changes in atmospheric chemistry to manipulate the climate system. Thus, in contrast to mitigation, which involves intentional manipulation of human action in order to minimize the unintentional impacts of human actions on the climate system, geoengineering involves strategies aimed at managing the climate system itself. Stated another way, addressing the problem via either adaptation or mitigation requires large elements of social innovation while addressing the problem via geoengineering depends primarily on scientific and technological innovation. This chapter explores the history of the debate surrounding geoengineering in order to understand the both the wave of interest in geoengineering and the likelihood that the wave will recede in the future.

In the final chapter, Western ideologies and values are discussed as being analogous to invasive exotic species to First Nation and Inuit cultures. Existing ecosystems are disrupted by Eurocentric-based ideas and laws about resource management, economic, legal, and socio-cultural systems to make way for oil and gas development. The impacts including the social, cultural, political, economic, and ecological destabilization of the Canadian North are discussed, as well as the growing threat of impacts from increased Arctic shipping due to climate change reducing ice cover.

Together, these chapters provide different views and responses to climate change, touching on resilience, adaptation, mitigation, cultural change, and our use of energy (both of the 'green' and fossil kind). The editors have selected these works as representative of the emerging debates and key issues within the field of environmental studies.

From a Cold Country: Climate Change, Cultural Sustainability and Canadian Cuisine

Dr. Lenore Newman,
Canada Research Chair, Food Security and Environment
Associate Professor, Department of Geography, University of the Fraser Valley
lenore.newman@ufv.ca

Introduction

As the Quebec folksong reminds us, *"Mon pays, ce n'est pas un pays, c'est l'hiver"*. Canada's national identity draws heavily on the wilderness and the frozen North of the imagination, and from ice hockey to skating on the Rideau Canal, winter is the season that captures our imagination. It is not surprising that our evolving culinary identity draws on regional specialties developed in areas with long, cold winters. However this link to wilderness and cold leaves Canadian specialties vulnerable to the effects of climate change. An examination of three iconic Canadian foods; ice wine, maple syrup, and salmon, suggest that adaptation will be necessary to guard against decreases in production of these key cultural icons. Potential disruption to iconic foods is a challenge for cultural sustainability that must be considered in sustainability plans.

Cuisine is a primary cultural signifier that contributes to our understanding of a place, and acts at many scales. Richards (2002) described gastronomy and cuisine as a significant source of identity formation and as a strong component of the "environmental bubble" in which tourists interact with the identity of a city, region or country. In short, cuisine matters at an economic level and at a deeper cultural level. Though cuisine is a critical element of culture, the sustainable

11

development discourse has had surprisingly little to say about it. Food security and sustainable agricultural systems are increasingly being raised as topics of interest to the sustainable development agenda, though aspects dealing with social and cultural sustainability are often dropped from the debate.

Exploration of culturally important crops and foods highlight one of the more insidious qualities of climate change. Critical crops and products are vulnerable to both general warming of the climate and an increase in extreme weather events, making climate change a "one-two punch". The IPCC (http://www.ipcc.ch/) predicts both accelerated warming and more extreme weather events for polar countries such as Canada. These two impacts acting in concert could compromise Canada's social and cultural food security, and even in cases where general warming increases productivity, extreme weather events can make reliable crop production and wild harvest difficult. A larger survey of Canada's food security in an age of climate change found three iconic foods that are particularly vulnerable to production disruption: ice wine, Pacific salmon, and maple syrup. Each food is explored in detail, but before I turn to the nuts and bolts of climate adaptation, it is interesting to ask whether iconic foods are important. Does a healthy cuisine lead to a sustainable society?

Social Sustainability and Cuisine

Access to culturally preferred foods is recognized as an important component of food security (Koç et al. 1999), and the idea of cultural food security must therefore be considered when food security is discussed as a component of community sustainability. However, of the "three pillars" of economic, ecological, and social/cultural sustainability, there is extensive literature exploring the difficulty of incorporating the social/cultural within sustainability discourses. As early as 1997, Throsby noted that sustainability and culture have sat awkwardly together, and Lehtonen observed in 2004 that the social aspect of

12

sustainability was the least discussed of the three pillars, particularly with respect to the social/environmental interface. As food production sits on this interface, the role of food production as a social and a cultural element of sustainable development remains poorly understood. Psarikido and Szerszynski (2012) claim that the social dimension of sustainability in food and agriculture is particularly neglected; Feenstra noted the need for a healthy food system as a component of community sustainability in 1997, and I extend this argument by contending that food security can be framed as a requirement for sustainable development. Cuisine and foodways can play a critical role in supporting social/cultural sustainable development. In the past I have framed sustainable development as a dynamic process (Newman, 2007) and this holds for cuisine as well; our culinary identity evolves and is strengthened by the availability of fresh regional ingredients, and this is only possible if two conditions are met; farmland and wild foodstocks much be healthy, and the social capital of harvesting groups must be healthy. Farming, for example, needs both land and a strong farm community, and both can be endangered by shocks to climate.

Benefits of a vibrant food system go beyond issues of hunger to issues of community building. If intact, cultural foodways are an element of community food security and thus of regional sustainability. We must thus ask whether Canada is at risk of losing key defining foods due to a rapidly changing climate. I see these cultural aspects of food security as elements of "soft infrastructure", a term used by Len Duhl at the University of California at Berkeley, which refers to community attributes that contribute to social well-being, including human services such as social services, recreation and culture. Soft infrastructure losses lead to less resilient communities (Dale and Newman 2009). Cuisine is an example of this critical element of culture; communities prosper economically from their iconic foods, and they also organize culturally around iconic foods. From the Salmon Festival in Steveston to the Maple Festival in Elmira, our foods are part of who we are.

Nationalism and Tertiary Food Security

As Benedict Anderson makes clear in his 2006 work, *Imagined Communities*, nations are complex constructs. Cultural material and symbolic artifacts are essential to nation-building projects; as well as highly visible symbols like language and religion, literature, music, art, and fashion. All of these elements are the stuff of nationalism, appropriated and repurposed as necessary by political elites. Cuisine is an increasingly important tool of nation building and of the construction of stable states (Cook and Crang 1996; Palmer 1998; Cusack 2000, 2004); well-known dishes can be used to represent national culture and to promote assimilation. Mintz (1996) has argued cuisines are inherently regional, but that they may be articulated nationally. The incorporation of the cuisine of each sub-region into the national cuisine is part of the creation of an integrated state; Bell and Valentine (1997) claim that the loss of iconic regional dishes can be viewed as the symbolic removal of support for the state. The construction of a national cuisine draws heavily on the landscape around it. The idea that a shifting culture is understudied in the sustainability and climate literatures, which focus on environment and economic impacts of climate change. There is, however, a long history behind the linkage of culture and landscape, for example (Makinder 1887) notes the link between societies and their surroundings. Landscapes have a physical reality, but also a mental and cultural one (Tress et al. 2001) and self-identity and group identity are tied to environment (Stephenson 2008). The link between environment and culture is in few places as clear as it is in the issue of cuisine. Food has been described as critical to the definition of group identity (Locher et al. 2005), helps to create the image of a place (Cook and Crang 1996), and has been explored as a cultural signifier on par with language (Bell and Valentine 1997). On a landscape level, food cuts across scales and is linked deeply to place; cuisines are examples of what Cook and Crang (1996) call "geographical knowledges", in which globally extensive flows of food, people, and knowledge are mediated locally. Cuisines are thus deeply embedded in place and help to determine regional and national identity.

The Enigma of Canadian Cuisine

The concept of a Canadian cuisine is evolving rapidly and poses a challenge to culinary researchers. Many factors influence cuisine, including gastronomic identity, geography and climate, and cultural elements such as religion, history, ethnic diversity, innovation, values and traditions (Harrington 2005). To further define Canadian cuisine in the context of concepts of the outdoors, winter, and wilderness, this project drew on data from the author's Canada Research Chair project, which involves both content analysis of menus, grey literature, web content such as food blogs, and an ongoing five-year field exploration of the country. Menu analysis in particular was used to identify iconic foods and trends. Menus from sites across the country were sampled longitudinally and then analyzed for both word frequency and for clustering effects in which certain terms occur together. Concurrent analysis of websites and blogs was compared with the first analysis, and in some cases interviews with chefs were used to tease out an understanding of why certain patterns predominate. Five strong themes have emerged so far; Canada's cuisine draws on seasonal foods, utilizes wild foods unusually heavily, highlights ingredients over recipes, is highly multicultural, and draws on regional specialties. These emerging themes are supported by what writing exists in the area: Jacobs (2009), for example, notes that although Canadian cuisine has proven difficult to define. He also notes that it combines the use of native ingredients with techniques and recipes that originated elsewhere. Canadian cuisine has also been described as one shaped by regions, climate, and cultural groups (Duncan 2003). Though a "national" cuisine remains elusive, these five themes serve as threads that run across our varied regions. Canada might be a country in search of a national food, but several strong contenders have certainly emerged.

Several authors have provided excellent guides to Canada's foods; Webb's 2008 work *Apples to Oysters* reflects the primacy of ingredients and the regional sweep and role of wild foods. She describes a country with many artisan producers, and long-standing traditions such as the gathering of wild dulse from the frigid waters of the Bay of Fundy. Dorothy Duncan writes of the changing seasons in *Nothing More Comforting* (2003) through foods such as rhubarb and maple syrup that mark out a rhythm to the year. She notes that both climate and cultural groups shape our complex culinary heritage. Books such as *Pemmican to Poutine* by Suman Roy and Brooke Ali (2010) follows similar themes of fresh, regional and wild foods, following writers such as Anita Stewart (2000, for example). More recently, the collection, *Edible Histories, Cultural Politics: Towards a Canadian Food History* by Iacovetta et al. (2012) notes growing interest in Canadian food. In that book for example, Hanrahan, notes the link to wild foods is very persistent; it is unusual for a cuisine to be so lightly rooted in agriculture.

In a study of farmers' markets across Canada (see Newman 2012), themes of fresh, local, and wild foods recurred in almost all regions of the country; it is little wonder that the "100 Mile Diet" (Smith and MacKinnon 2007) is Canadian. This craving for the fresh and local ties deeply to our continued engagement with seasonality; though we are no longer as constrained by seasonal availability of foods, there is a strong sense of seasonality within Canadian cuisine that expresses not as the seasonal availability of foods, but as the consumption of foods in the season in which they are traditionally harvested. While working at the Vancouver Farmer's Market location at Trout Lake, Vancouver, I was surprised by how keen the average person's internal seasonal clock really was; we had a late season in 2011due to rain, and people would impatiently ask us each week where the blueberries were. They knew it was time for blueberries! A study conducted by Wilkins et al. (2000) supports this anecdote, and found not only that almost all participants could name local seasonal foods, but also that 78 percent of participants only ate these foods when they were fresh locally. This passion for fresh and local foods helps to maintain the regional focus of Canadian cuisine, though this is perhaps less clear than it once was; many mainstays are now appearing across the country; however statistical data still reflects higher consumption of wild foods such as salmon, moose and berries in the regions where these foods are found. Wild foods tie into a generally strong link between food and the outdoors in Canada. Morel (2008) notes that Canadians eat outdoors and conduct wild provisioning as part of their concept of commensality. When we are pouring maple syrup onto snow or grilling salmon over an open fire, we are engaged in creating a culinary habitus that embraces the scope of Canada's wild, if only through brief engagement with the outdoors.

Our connection to winter, cold, and wilderness might help to make us Canadian, but it also makes Canadian cuisine particularly vulnerable to changes in climate. As a Northern country, Canada is expected to suffer large shifts in climate due to anthropogenic climate change, including warmer winters, warmer night temperatures, and hotter summers (McBean and Henstra 2012). In addition to this gradual change, Canada is expected to experience an increase in extreme events, including more frequent floods, droughts, and ice storms (McBean and Henstra 2012). These changes pose a challenge both to farmers and to wild foodstocks; our management of land will need to change, and our social support of farmers and gatherers will need to strengthen. But what might the impacts to individual foods look like?

As noted above the project methodology involved first identifying iconic Canadian foods and then selecting a subset of those foods likely to be impacted by climate change. The selection was made through a grey literature analysis of websites, blogs, and various writing about food, cross referencing with the primary author's field notes, as well as analysis of online menus conducted by the author to identify both word frequency and word cluster effects. Content analysis indentified key ingredients and elements advertized as central to the Canadian culinary experience. The larger project identified several economically and culturally important foods, though this discussion highlights only the three that appeared most often on menus across the country: maple syrup, salmon, and ice wine. Hashimoto and Telfer (2006) call maple syrup and smoked salmon the stereotypical Canadian foods, a stereotype that certainly appears to be an accurate reflection. These three products appeared in all regions of the country, and maple in particular appears on a great number of menus

17

year round and can appear in almost any course of the meal. Salmon was an option on over three quarters of the menus analyzed, even in land-locked regions. Ice wine is more of a newcomer, but has emerged as a high quality Canadian food export. It is important to note this method highlights our public cuisine, the foods we present to the world in our restaurants and as cultural products. It is unlikely many Canadians sit down regularly to a meal of maple-glazed salmon and ice wine, though that sounds rather appealing.

Maple Syrup and Climate Adaptation

Canada's best known iconic national food, maple syrup, is a major part of our folklore, and an important income generator in rural areas of Quebec and Eastern Ontario. Maple syrup also appears in menus across the country as an ingredient used as part of any course served at any time of the day. Quebec produces 80% of the world's supply of maple syrup, and in a world where food conscious consumers are questioning the safety of sweeteners such as high fructose corn syrup, demand for maple products is continuing to rise. Though most of Canada's maple syrup is consumed in North America, Japan is also a key market for the crop as maple enjoys popularity there and in Korea as well. Made from the sap of the *Acer Saccharum*, or sugar maple, maple syrup and maple sugar provide on average one quarter of the annual income of small producers. This income comes before planting season, and can be critical in the sustainability of rural farming (Hinrichs 1998). There are roughly 13,500 producers in Quebec, and the industry produces 610 million in GDP. This regional focus, however, downplays the role maple plays in national cuisine, and maple syrup is easily the best-known iconic Canadian food.

Maple syrup and sugar is native to North America, and before colonization, maple syrup and maple sugar were important foods of both the indigenous peoples who produced these foods and those who traded for them. These products were labour intensive, but the indigenous people in maple regions produced both sugar and syrup, concentrating the sap in hollowed logs either through freezing the sap and discarding the water ice, or boiling the sap with hot stones. Maple sugar production was done on a large scale and the sugar, which was much easier to pack than syrup, was used in a widespread maple trade. Locally meat was boiled in syrup to give it flavour (Mason 1990). European settlers quickly joined the trade in maple syrup and maple sugar, as conventional sugar sources were unavailable or prohibitively expensive.

Maple syrup remained popular in North America despite the difficulty of production in part because of politics; in the United States, maple products were seen as necessary to creating independence from Britain's sugar trade. In Canada, the desire to use a sugar untainted by slavery created an increased market for maple products. The abolitionist movement described maple as being "more pleasant and more patriotic than that ground by the hand of slavery" (Pierce 2002). Sugaring thus remained a common activity and has endured in areas where it is economically important and where it is an economically marginal activity, as it both emerges from and helps create the local community culture and resource environment (Hinrichs 1998). Today maple appears across the country as a sweetener, and as a flavouring agent. At one end of the culinary scale is the quotidian experience offered by Tim Horton's maple glazed donuts. At the other end of the culinary map is the modern version of the *cabane a sucre*; for example the feasts designed by chef Martin Picard of the Montreal restaurant *Au Pied de Cochon* at his Miribel sugar bush features a menu changed daily. One evening's feast included confit duck drumsticks in a maple reduction, maple whiskey, and maple cured ham, though the meal also featured the more traditional preparation of maple syrup poured onto snow. From maple sugar pie to the "Hello Kitty" brand bottles of maple syrup sold at Vancouver International Airport (see Figure 1a), maple is the flavour most often linked to our national identity.

Figure 1a. Hello Kitty Maple Syrup

Photo by Lenore Newman

Maple syrup production is particularly vulnerable to climate change. First, the tree roots require snow cover for protection. Declining snow cover exposes the trees to sudden freezes, damaging the trees and lowering sap production. Second, the short production season is easily disrupted by extreme climate events. The syrup season only lasts four to six weeks in the early spring, when temperatures crossing back and forth across the freezing point cause the sap in the trees to run freely. In the last fifteen years, sap production has declined as April temperatures have risen. It is estimated that the industry will decline by about 20% in the next forty years; decline in the US will be much sharper. Extreme weather can also pose a threat to syrup production, the 1998 ice storm destroyed 12.5% of the taps in Eastern Ontario, and dropped syrup production by 25% for a cost of 2.9 million in damage and 4.2 million in lost revenue (Kidon et al. 2001). Adapting the industry will require opening up areas in Quebec to the north of the current regions of production. 17% of Quebec's commercial forest is sugar maple, and only a small portion of that is used for sugaring. However, such a move will not help small farmers facing declining production in the South, and a lack of access to Quebec's remote regions will hinder expansion.

20

Climate Adaptation and the Canadian Ice Wine Industry

Canada's ice wine industry is a testament to our increasingly talented wine industry. It is possibly the most internationally renowned variety of wine from Canada, and despite the limited annual yield is an economically important and culturally valuable product. Ice wine is a sweet dessert wine made from grapes harvested when frozen on the vine, and ice wine production, like the production of maple syrup, requires specific weather and temperature conditions, leaving this product vulnerable to climate change. Though warmer summer temperatures can boost grape production and increase sugar content, a longer wait for freezing leads to greater moisture losses to evaporation and leaves the crops vulnerable to predation by hungry birds. Most of the world's ice wine comes from Germany, Canada, and Austria, although ice wine is also produced in countries such as France, Italy, Hungary, Slovenia, and Switzerland (Rolle et al. 2010). Canada has become the world's largest producer of ice wine (Cyr and Kusy 2007), a status it has achieved as a result of the inherent climatic conditions necessary for ice wine production: Germany, formerly the world's leading ice wine producer, cannot guarantee a crop every year. Canada is the only major ice wine producing country that can guarantee an annual crop of frozen grapes (Lawlor 2010), a guarantee challenged by climate change. Though the wine has an international stature as a Canadian iconic product, only small areas of Canada have a climate suited to the growing and harvesting of grapes in general, and a smaller area of our grape growing regions are suitable for ice wine. Changing temperature or weather pattern changes within these areas has the potential to affect the quality, flavour, and yield of frozen wine grapes.

Canada's success is partly due to exacting standards for production. In Canada, the VQA requires that grapes be naturally frozen on the vine at -8°C or colder and that this temperature be maintained throughout the pressing process without artificial refrigeration (Rolle et al. 2010). Further, the sugar content must meet a certain standard, requiring exacting weather conditions (Subden et al. 2003). Thus far, only wines from British Columbia and Ontario have managed to meet the standards required for VQA labelling. The main wine grape growing regions in Canada comprise the Niagara Peninsula and the adjacent areas of Pelee Island and the north shore of Lake Erie in Ontario, along with the Okanagan and Similkameen Valleys in British Columbia (Shaw 2009). The location of the Niagara Peninsula between the cooler waters of Lake Ontario to the north and the eastern end of Lake Erie to the south exposes the region to strong lake breezes that help to cool the summer temperatures, while the lakes act as heat sinks that warm the air in the winter (Shaw 2005).

Climate change has the potential to badly disrupt ice wine production. The successful cultivation of wine grapes requires even heat, protection from sudden frost, and protection from extreme heat and excessive freezing and thawing cycles (White et al. 2006). Although many individual climate factors, including solar radiation, wind, and humidity, play a role in yield formation, grape development and grape composition, Schultz and Jones (2010) found that temperature and water supply are among the most important. Changes in climatic conditions that jeopardize any of these climatic factors, particularly temperature and temperature extremes, pose high risk for ice wine producers (Cyr and Kusy 2007). Currently, many wine producing regions are under threat from climate change; a study by White et al. (2006) found that the area available for production of premium wine grapes in the United States will both contract and shift over the next century. Climate change is manifesting in increasing mean temperatures, altered precipitation patterns, greater frequency of temperature extremes, and increased climatic variability (Holland and Smit 2010), all of these factors are of concern for ice wine production. Increasing mean temperatures are opening up new areas to viticulture, hence the emerging wine regions in Quebec and Nova Scotia. Although these provinces are known for short, cool summers and cold winters, the effects of climate change are rendering areas within the provinces more conducive to wine grapes (Shaw 1999).

Disruption of ice wine production is of specific concern as it is more difficult than the production of other wines to begin with. Because grapes must be pressed while frozen; the juice yield from ice wine grape pressing is only 15% to 20% by volume of what the same grapes would have produced if destined for table wine (Cyr and Kusy 2007). The scarcity of ice wine in relation to demand is part of the reason it can command such a high price in relation to table wine. While Canada currently benefits from being the only ice wine producing country that can guarantee annual temperatures low enough to produce an adequate supply of frozen grapes, if mean temperatures increase to the point where winter temperature conditions are not optimal for ice wine production Canadian producers will experience significant value loss. The major risk faced by producers is that a mild winter with relatively high daily temperatures can result in grapes being harvested later in the winter months which puts them at much greater risk of deterioration from wind, rot, and other factors (Cyr and Kusy 2007).

In the long term increasing mean temperatures will pose the greatest risk to the Canadian ice wine industry, but climate variability is immediately responsible for the greatest risk of value and production loss (Cyr and Kusy 2007). Because of the inherently regional nature and specific climatic requirements of production, it does not lend itself to a shift in cultivation location. While climate change has the potential to increase yields and quality of ice wine grapes, and thus the value of ice wine to producers, both temperature extremes due to climate variability and significant increases in mean winter temperatures have the potential to cause significant losses in value and yields.

Pacific Salmon and Climate Adaptation

Aside from maple syrup, salmon is the best-known Canadian food, perhaps explaining why maple-glazed salmon is one of the most common dishes found in restaurants across the country. Salmon play an important role in both the cuisine and the culture of Canada's West Coast, and is a critical cultural food for both indigenous populations and for newcomers. On the East Coast, Salmon are no longer as common, but still remain a storied sport fish. Indigenous groups of British Columbia relied heavily on salmon to sustain complex societies, and large fixed settlements, and dried salmon in both stick form and processed into pemmican was traded far inland from the coast. Settlements were established near salmon rivers and streams, and the development of technologies for fishing, processing, and storing salmon led to the increasing permanence of these coastal settlements, which in turn allowed the development of sophisticated stone and plant technologies and complex social organizations (Muckle 2007).

Newcomers to the West Coast quickly found themselves dependent on the salmon as well. When settlers colonized Indigenous territories, they also began fishing salmon. In the 1870s colonial salmon fisheries began building export markets, and large industrial fishing operations were established to supply both to local and global markets (Schreiber 2006). Traditional Indigenous dishes such as smoked salmon became popular among the West Coast population, as did fusion dishes that incorporate salmon into immigrant cuisines. In particular salmon has been incorporated into Vancouver-style sushi to a degree where it plays a role equal only to tuna as an ingredient. Salmon has been branded as a traditional Canadian food, and in turn has been used to brand British Columbia (Hashimoto and Telfer 2006). Smoked salmon is sold alongside maple syrup at tourist shops, both resulting from and further increasing its reputation as a traditional Canadian food. Further, the importance of salmon as a source of protein is growing, increasing demand for the fish (Gerwing and McDaniels 2006). Perhaps the best example of the ubiquity of salmon in British Columbian food culture comes from the BC roll, a variety of maki sushi extremely common in restaurants on the West Coast, featuring barbecued or grilled salmon along with cucumber and a sweet sauce.

Figure 1b. Granville Island smoked salmon display

Photo by Lenore Newman.

There are five distinct species of Pacific salmon, and all are fished in British Columbia: Chinook, chum, coho, pink, and sockeye. In the wild, all five of the species of Pacific salmon are born in freshwater lakes or streams, make their way out to the saltwater seas, and after anywhere between one and five years, depending on their species they return to their natal stream to spawn. This makes salmon more vulnerable to climate change than many other fish; they are impacted by ocean level changes and by changes in the much more sensitive environment of streams, rivers, and lakes. Pacific salmon are extremely adaptable in some ways; the biological characteristics of a given salmon stock can evolve dramatically in only a few generations in response to environmental changes (Johnsen 2010). However, despite the inherent adaptability of salmon, runs have decreased dramatically due to habitat destruction and overfishing. Beamish (1995) claims that these variations are rarely random; they are dependent on the external factors, such as fisheries, climate, and ecosystem. Even though wild salmon stocks are declining, there has been an increased consumer demand for salmon within Canada, leading to a growing farming industry. Salmon farming, however, is highly contentious; there is significant evidence of environmental harm stemming from this industry, including additional damage to wild salmon stocks. Further, many of the coastal First Nations oppose the industry, as it threatens the destruction of their traditional ways of life (Page 2007). Many Indigenous people argue that rather than establishing fish farms, the focus should be on protecting the environment and caring for the ecosystem of wild Pacific salmon (Gerwing and McDaniels 2006). In addition, farming is also subject to changing ocean temperatures and conditions associated with climate change.

Pacific salmon face threats on numerous fronts. Temperature changes, reductions in summer flows, increased winter flooding, and increased sedimentation are all among the threats caused by climate change (Miller 2000). In terms of the threats posed to Pacific salmon from climate change, temperature has been identified as one of the most essential factors to survival. Temperatures that are either too high or too low are lethal, although temperature resistance is based upon adaptation. Tolerance of extremes of either high or low temperatures is based on previous temperature history (Brett 1952). Temperature affects salmon differently depending on the stage they are at in their life cycle, although they are most vulnerable at the same stages when they are in freshwater (Beacham and Murray 1990; Mantua et al. 1997). Many streams once inhabited by large salmon runs are now at lethal temperatures; salmon are considered extinct in 142 watershed systems throughout British Columbia where they are traditionally found (Slaney et al. 1996; Price et al. 2008). Even where salmon populations can adapt to higher temperatures, infection rates and virulence of fish pathogens increase and lessen the ability of a fish to withstand disease (Richter and Kolmes 2005). Spring and Coho salmon are most resistant to high temperatures, while pink and chum salmon are least resistance. Sockeye salmon are distinguishable from the other two only by greater resistance to prolonged exposure to high temperatures, though none of these species can tolerate temperatures above 25.1 degrees Celsius (Brett 1952).

Protection of streams and rivers, and management of their water levels and temperatures, will be critical to the survival of salmon in British Columbia. Warmer atmospheric temperatures associated with climate change are predicted to continue reducing winter snowfall, thus contributing to significant summer flow reductions in all streams and rivers that depend on melting snow. River flows are expected to increase in the winter, resulting from the increase in rainfall relative to snowfall also concomitant to warmer atmospheric temperatures, and strong currents pose a risk to salmon roe. However, decreased summer flows pose a much greater threat to Pacific salmon, and are associated with lower survival rates. Both increased winter flows and decreased summer flows pose risks to the ecosystem surrounding both Pacific salmon and the freshwater streams and rivers in which they can be found, as they affect the surrounding forests and other plant life (Mote et al. 2003).

The life cycle of the salmon is closely tied to the health of the temperate rainforest of British Columbia. Salmon die shortly after spawning, and their decaying bodies release nutrients into the water and the surrounding forest. The amounts of both organic nutrients and inorganic particulate matter in natal streams are lower following small salmon runs, and are believed to contribute to lower survival rates for the next generation of Pacific salmon (Rex and Petticrew 2008). This risk is compounded by the increasing sedimentation of rivers and streams associated with climate change. Warmer winter temperatures and increased flows during the cool period, when flows are naturally at their highest, increase sedimentation. Higher levels of sedimentation are associated with decreased chances of embryo survival (Crouse et al. 1981).

Long-term projections for Pacific salmon are extremely poor without significant effort to adapt the species to changing environments. Fishers and communities in British Columbia are often recommended to decrease economic reliance on salmon (Mote et al. 2003). Strategies to release young salmon into streams and rivers raise community awareness about salmon habitats; however, they have not had significant impacts on salmon runs (Beamish 1995). Temperature variability and increased atmospheric temperatures, reductions of summer flows and enlarged winter flows, and increased sedimentation are among the greatest climate change-related risks to salmon (Miller 2000). Streams must be protected and where possible shaded to maintain water temperature, and decisions over water use might need to favour salmon over energy, agriculture and domestic use. The survival of Pacific salmon, and the ecosystem that supports them, must be considered in any decision affecting watersheds in British Columbia.

Conclusions

The impact of global environmental change upon regional and national cuisines is an understudied area of the sustainable development literature, and this initial study of the Canadian context suggests the potential for significant economic and cultural disruptions if mitigation strategies are not enacted to protect iconic foods. Though Canada's well developed food infrastructure is likely to prevent any serious disruption of primary and secondary food security, it is possible that certain iconic foods within the cuisine could be seriously disrupted, damaging the soft infrastructure that such foods and cuisines add to regional and national economies and cultures. Disruptions can be categorized into an increase in extreme events that can cause one-time damage, and long-term challenges posed by rising temperature; farmers and policy makers will need to be cognizant of both. Canada is well placed to maintain a robust food industry in the face of a shifting climate, but advance planning will be required if the farm base is to weather the potential economic and physical challenges created by a changing world. Production of the three foods highlighted here requires specialized knowledge and intensive human capital that is not easily regained once destroyed; a precautionary approach to protecting these culinary elements is thus preferable to reactive policies that compensate for damage after the fact.

Maple production is particularly vulnerable to climate change, and the only effective long-term adaptation method will be to establish production regions North of current production zones. This will not protect current producers, leaving them vulnerable to economic impacts. Ice wine producers will be in a similar situation, and will require improved protection from extreme weather events, either through crop innovation or improved insurance regimes. Salmon production will require more diligent river protection, including shading programs and careful monitoring of water levels. Vigorous habitat improvement will be effective in the medium term, though if climate change remains unchecked the industry will eventually move North. Though Canada certainly has the potential to benefit from a Northward shift in production of many foods, one has to remember that our infrastructure is concentrated along the Southern border of the country. New producers in Northern regions would need transportation infrastructure, processing capacity, and would of course be much farther from their target markets in major cities.

Failure to meet these challenges will weaken the cultural soft infrastructure of the country and its regions, impacting important economic chains and weakening important community traditions and rituals. As Canada is a nation undergoing rapid change and a related shift in national identity, the loss of key culinary elements could be particularly disruptive. The loss of social and cultural capital has been poorly characterized in the sustainable development discourse, but preservation of cuisines and regional foodways is of importance to meeting the objectives of community sustainability. Preserving cuisines and regional foodways should be understood both as an end in itself and also as a component of community sustainability; however, the precarious situation of fundamental building blocks of Canadian cuisine, including but not limited to the ingredients discussed herein, also present an opportunity to rethink communication around climate change. If cuisine is a component of nationalism and nationhood, and if Canadian cuisine is under threat from climate change, is the Canadian nation not under threat? Understanding nations as constructions, the building blocks of the cuisine that is itself a building block of Canada are under threat. Perhaps Canada can outlive maple syrup, ice wine, and Pacific salmon, yet the idea of what Canada is will likewise have to adapt. If climate adaptation and mitigation strategies are not quickly implemented, adaptation and mitigation will have to be writ at the level of the nation.

Acknowledgements

I would like to acknowledge the assistance of Katherine Burnett in the research for this project, and I would like to acknowledge that this project was partially funded by the Social Science and Humanities Research Council of Canada.

References

Anderson, Benedict. 2006. *Imagined Communities: Reflections on the Origin and Spread of Nationalism*. London: Verso.

Beacham, Terry D., and Clyde B. Murray. "Temperature, egg size, and development of embryos and alevins of five species of Pacific salmon: a comparative analysis." *Transactions of the American Fisheries Society* 119, no. 6 (1990): 927-945.

Beamish, R. J. 1995. "Introduction - The Need to Understand the Relationship Between Climate and the Dynamics of Fish Populations." In *Climate change and northern fish* populations, edited by R. J. Beamish, 1-2. Ottawa: National Research Council of Canada.

Bell, David, and Gill Valentine. 1997. *Consuming Geographies*. London: Routledge.

Brett, John Roland. 1952. "Temperature Tolerance in Young Pacific Salmon, Genus Oncorhynchus." *Journal of the Fisheries Board of Canada* 9:265-323.

Cook, Ian, and Phillip Crang. 1996. "The World on a Plate: Culinary Culture, Displacement, and Geographical Knowledges." *Journal of Material Culture* 1:131-153

Crouse, M. R., C. A. Callahan, K. W. Malueg, and S. E. Dominguez. 1981. "Effects of Fine Sediments on Growth of Juvenile Coho Salmon in Laboratory Streams." *Transactions of the American Fisheries Society* 110:81-286.

Cusack, Igor. 2000. "African Cuisines: Recipes for Nationbuilding?" *Journal of African Cultural Studies* 13: 207-225.

Cusack, Igor. 2004. "'Equatorial Guinea's National Cuisine is Simple and Tasty': Cuisine and the Making of National Culture."

Arizona Journal of Hispanic Cultural Studies 8:131-149.

Cyr, Don, and Martin Kusy. 2007. "Canadian Ice Wine Production: A Case for the Use of Weather Derivatives." *Journal of Wine Economics* 2:145-167.

Dale, Ann, and Lenore Newman. 2009. "Sustainable Development for Some: "Green" Urban Development and Affordability." *Local Environment* 14:669-683.

Duncan, Dorothy. 2003. *Nothing More Comforting: Canada's Heritage Food.* Dundurn Group: Toronto.

Feenstra, Gail W. 1997. "Local Food Systems and Sustainable Communities." *American Journal of Alternative Agriculture* 12:28-36.

Gerwing, Kira, and Timothy McDaniels. 2006. "Listening to the Salmon People: Coastal First Nations' Objectives Regarding Salmon Aquaculture in British Columbia." *Society and Natural Resources* 19:259-273.

Hanrahan, Maura. 2012. *Pine-clad hills and spindrift swirl: The character, persistence, and significance of rural Newfoundland foodways.* in Iacovetta, Frank, Korinek, Valerie, & Epp, Marlene (2012) *Edible Histories, Cultural Politics: Towards a Canadian Food History.* Toronto: University of Toronto Press. pp. 85-93.

Harrington, Robert J. 2006. "Defining Gastronomic Identity." *Journal of Culinary Science & Technology* 4:129-152.

Hashimoto, Atsuko, and David J. Telfer. "Selling Canadian Culinary Tourism: Brand and the Global and the Regional Product." *Tourism Geographies* 8:31-55.

Hinrichs, C. Claire. 1998. "Sideline and Lifeline: The Cultural Economy of Maple Syrup Production." *Rural Sociology* 63:507-532.

Hjalager, Anne-Mette, and Greg Richards, eds. 2002. *Tourism and gastronomy.* London: Routledge.

Holland, T., and B. Smit. 2010. "Climate Change and the Wine Industry: Current Research Themes and New Directions." *Journal of Wine Research* 21:125-136.

Iacovetta, F., Korinek, Valerie, & Epp, Marlene. 2012. *Edible Histories, Cultural Politics: Towards a Canadian Food History.* Toronto:

University of Toronto Press.

Jacobs, Hersch. 2009. "Structural Elements in Canadian Cuisine." *Cuizine: The Journal of Canadian Food Culture* 2. Accessed June 14, 2010. doi:10.7202/039510ar.

Johnsen, D. Bruce. 2010. "Salmon, Science, and Reciprocity on the Northwest Coast." *Ecology & Society* 14:10-14.

Kindon, Jennifer, Glenn Fox, Dan McKenney, and Kimberly Rollins. 2001. "Economic Impact of the 1998 Ice Storm on the Eastern Ontario Maple Syrup Industry." *The Forestry Chronicle* 77:667-675.

Koç, Mustafa, Rod MacRae, Luc J. A. Mougeot, and Jennifer Welsh. 1999. *For Hunger-Proof Cities: Sustainable Urban Food Systems*. Ottawa: IDRC.

Lawlor, Julia. 2010. "Frozen Vines (and Fingers) Yield a Sweet Reward." *New York Times*, February 26:32.

Lehtonen, Markku. 2004. "The Environmental-Social Interface of Sustainable Development: Capabilities, Social Capital, Institutions." *Ecological Economics* 49: 199-214.

Locher, Julie L., William C. Yoels, Donna Maurer, Jillian van Ells. 2005. "Comfort Foods: an Exploratory Journey into the Social and Emotional Significance of Food." *Food and Foodways* 13:273-297.

Makinder, H. J. 1887. "On the Scope and Methods of Geography." *Proceedings of the Royal Geographical Society and Monthly Record of Geography* 9:141-160.

Mantua, Nathan J., Steven R. Hare, Yuan Zhang, John M. Wallace, and Robert C. Francis. 1997. "A Pacific Interdecadal Climate Oscillation with Impacts on Salmon Production." *Bulletin of the American Meteorological Society* 78:1069-1079.

Mason, Carol I. 1990. "A Sweet Small Something: Maple Sugaring in the New World." In *The Invented Indian: Cultural Fictions and Government Policies*, edited by James A. Clifton, 91-106. New Brunswick: Transaction Publishers.

McBean, Gordon and Dan Henstra. 2009. *Climate Change Adaptation and Extreme Weather*. Vancouver: Simon Fraser University. Accessed June 14, 2020. http://act-adapt.org/wp-content/uploads/2011/03/PDFWeatherSession_SummaryReport. pdf

Miller, Kathleen A. 2000. "Pacific Salmon Fisheries: Climate, Information and Adaptation in a Conflict-Ridden Context." *Climatic Change* 45:37-61.

Mintz, Sidney W. 1996. *Tasting Food, Tasting Freedom: Excursions into Eating, Culture, and the Past*. Boston: Beacon Press.

Morel, Pauline. 2008. "Eating Out: The Influence of the Outdoors on Canadian Domestic Foodways." Paper presented at Domestic Foodscapes: Towards Mindful Eating?, Montreal, Quebec, March 21-22. Cited with permission.

Mote, Philip W., Edward A. Parson, Alan F. Hamlet, William S. Keeton, Dennis Lettenmaier, Nathan Mantua, Edward L. Miles, David W. Peterson, Richard Slaughter, and Amy K. Snover. 2003. "Preparing for Climatic Change: The Water, Salmon, and Forests of the Pacific Northwest." *Climatic Change* 61:45-88.

Muckle, Robert James. 2007. *The First Nations of British Columbia: An Anthropological Survey*. Vancouver: University of British Columbia Press.

Newman, Lenore. 2012. "Neige et Citrouille: Seasonality in a Canadian Urban Market." *CuiZine: The Journal of Canadian Food Cultures* 3. Accessed June 14, 2010. doi: 10.7202/1012453ar

Newman, Lenore. 2007. " The virtuous cycle: Incremental changes and a process-based sustainable development" *Sustainable Development* 15: 267-274.

Page, Justin. 2007. "Salmon Farming in First Nations' Territories: A Case of Environmental Injustice on Canada's West Coast." *Local Environment* 12:613-626.

Palmer, Catherine. 1998. "From Theory to Practice: Experiencing the Nation in Everyday Life." *Journal of Material Culture* 3:175-199.

Pierce, A. 2002. "Maple syrup (acer saccharrum)". In P. Shanley, A. Pierce, S. Laird, & A. Guillen (Eds.), *Tapping the green market: Certification and management of non-timber forest products* (162-171). London, UK: Earthscan Publications.

Price, M. H. H., C. T. Darlmont, N. F. Temple, and S. M. MacDuffee.

2008. "Ghost Runs: Management and Status Assessment of Pacific Salmon (Oncorhynchus spp.) Returning to British Columbia's Central and North Coasts." *Canadian Journal Of Fisheries & Aquatic Sciences* 65:2712-2718.

Psarikidou, Katerina and Szerszynski Bronislaw. 2012. "Growing the Social: Alternative Agrifood Networks and Social Sustainability in the Urban Ethical Foodscape." *Sustainability: Science, Practice, & Policy* 8:30-39.

Rex, John F. and Ellen L. Petticrew. 2008. "Delivery of Marine-Derived Nutrients to Streambeds by Pacific Salmon." *Nature Geoscience* 1:840-843.

Richards, Greg. 2002. "Gastronomy: An Essential Ingredient in Tourism Production and Consumption." In *Tourism and Gastronomy*, edited by Hjalager, A and Greg Richards, 3-20. London and New York: Routledge.

Richter, Ann, and Steven A. Kolmes. 2005. "Maximum Temperature Limits for Chinook, Coho, and Chum Salmon, and Steelhead Trout in the Pacific Northwest." *Reviews in Fisheries Science* 13:23-49.

Rolle, Luca, Fabrizio Torchio, Simone Giacosa, and Vincenzo Gerbi. 2009. "Modifications of Mechanical Characteristics and Phenolic Composition in Berry Skins and Seeds of Mondeuse Winegrapes throughout the On-Vine Drying Process." *Journal of the Science of Food and Agriculture* 89:1973-1980.

Roy, Suman, and Brooke Ali. 2010. *From Pemmican to Poutine: A Journey through Canada's Culinary History*. Toronto: Key Publishing House.

Schreiber, Dorothee. 2006. "First Nations, Consultation, and the Rule of Law: Salmon Farming and Colonialism in British Columbia." *American Indian culture and research journal* 30:19-40.

Schultz, Hans R., and Gregory V. Jones. 2010. "Climate Induced Historic and Future Changes in Viticulture." *Journal of Wine Research* 21:137-145.

Schultz, H. R., and Manfred Stoll. 2009. "Some Critical Issues in Environmental Physiology of Grapevines: Future Challenges and Current Limitations." *Australian Journal of Grape and Wine*

Research 16:4-24.

Shaw, Anthony B. 2009. "The Emerging Cool Climate Wine Regions of Eastern Canada." *Journal of wine research* 10:79-94.

Shaw, Anthony B. 2005. "The Niagara Peninsula Viticultural Area: A Climatic Analysis of Canada's Largest Wine Region." *Journal of Wine Research* 16:85-103.

Slaney, T. L., K. D. Hyatt, T. G. Northcot, and R. J. Fielden. 1996. "Status of Anadromous Salmon and Trout in British Columbia and Yukon." *Fisheries* 21:20-38.

Smith, Alisa, and James Bernard MacKinnon. 2008. *The 100-Mile Diet: A Year of Local Eating.* New York: Random House.

Stephenson, Janet. 2008. "The Cultural Values Model: An Integrated Approach to Values in Landscapes." *Landscape and Urban Planning* 84:127-139.

Stewart, Anita. 2000. *The Flavours of Canada: A Celebration of the Finest Regional Foods*
Vancouver: Raincoast Books.

Subden, R. E., J. I. Husnik, R. Van Twest, G. Van Der Merwe, and H. J. J. van Vuuren. 2003. "Autochthonous Microbial Population in a Niagara Peninsula Icewine Must." *Food Research International* 36:747-751.

Throsby, David. 1997. "Sustainability and Culture: Some Theoretical Issues." *International Journal of Cultural Policy* 4:7-19.

Tress, Bärbel, Gunther Tress, Henri Décamps, and Anne-Marie d'Hauteserre. 2001. "Bridging Human and Natural Sciences in Landscape Research." *Landscape and Urban Planning* 57:137-141.

Webb, Margaret. 2009. *Apples to Oysters: A Food Lover's Tour of Canadian Farms.* Toronto: Penguin.

White, Michael A., N. S. Diffenbaugh, Gregory V. Jones, J. S. Pal, and F. Giorgi. 2006. "Extreme Heat Reduces and Shifts United States Premium Wine Production in the 21st Century." *Proceedings of the National Academy of Sciences* 103:11217-11222.

Wilkins, Jennifer L., Elizabeth Bowdish, and Jeffery Sobal. 2000, "University Student Perceptions of Seasonal and Local Foods." *Journal of Nutrition Education* 32:261-268.

Building resilience and adaptive capacity through Farmer-Managed Natural Regeneration in Africa: Lessons from two case studies

H. Carolyn Peach Brown
Environmental Studies
University of Prince Edward Island
Charlottetown, PEI, Canada
hcpbrown@upei.ca

Maggie Ibrahim
Resilience Manager
World Vision UK
London, UK
Maggie.Ibrahim@worldvision.org.uk

Nicola Ward
Adaptation Learning Programme for Africa (ALP)
CARE International
nward@careclimatechange.org

Introduction

Africa, the continent considered to have contributed the least amount of greenhouse gases to the atmosphere, will experience the impacts of climate change most acutely. Living in the poorest region in the world, in economic terms, African populations are expected to be more vulnerable to climate change as a result of the interaction of three factors: a higher than the global average degree of change in climate, high levels of dependence on agriculture and natural resources, forest goods and services, and a low degree of adaptive capacity (Eastaugh 2010; Toulmin 2009). Adaptive capacity refers to the potential or capability of a system to adjust to and thereby limit risk (Adger and Vincent 2005; Smit and Wandel 2006). Adaptive capacity is often limited due to a lack of key determinants such as economic wealth, technology, information and skills, infrastructure, institutions, social capital and equity (Smit and Pilifosova 2001, 2003). Climate change impacts, such as that on water resources, forests and food production, will likely further exacerbate poverty and hinder the achievement of the Millennium Development Goals.

Recognition of the need to address climate change in tandem with other development efforts is now prevalent in many development aid agencies and non-governmental organizations (NGOs) (Mitchell and van Aalst 2008; Mitchell and Tanner 2006; McGray, Hammill, and Bradley 2007). World Vision (WV), a Christian relief, development and advocacy organization dedicated to working with the world's most vulnerable people, especially children, to help them improve their well-being is one such NGO. Established in 1950 to care for orphans in Asia, WV has grown to embrace the larger issues of community development, humanitarian relief, and advocacy for the poor in its mission to help children and their families build sustainable futures. The organization assists some 100 million people in nearly 100 countries, focusing on human and social transformation (World Vision International 2013, 2008, 2011).

In light of the potential of climate change to negatively impact child well-being, their key indicator of success, WV's international partnership office began addressing climate change issues in 2006 through what is now called the Climate Change Response Initiative (CCRI) (World Vision International 2010). Through its integrated development programmes, WV has been seeking to build local adaptive capacity for a range of shocks, stresses and trends, including conflict, droughts, food insecurity, floods and environmental decline (Ibrahim and Ward 2012; Brown, Brown, and Shore 2014). One approach has sought to build adaptive capacity through addressing unsustainable land management through Farmer-Managed Natural Regeneration (FMNR) on degraded land in Ghana and Ethiopia. Through two case studies, this chapter will explore the challenges and successes of this approach and the role that it can play in enhancing adaptive capacity and fostering resilience to climate change in the developing world. First the literature related to resilience and adaptive capacity is briefly reviewed including an explanation of the Local Adaptive Capacity framework used for analysis in this chapter. Following a review of the concept of FMNR, the context

37

of the case studies and methodology are explained. Next, the results of case study analysis of each aspect of the LAC framework are presented. We end with a discussion of the results in the context of the broader literature on international development and climate change.

Resilience and Adaptive Capacity

Building the capacity to adapt to change in social-ecological systems is a common theme across disciplines. Adaptive capacity refers to the potential or capability of a system to adjust to and thereby limit risk (Adger and Vincent 2005; Smit and Wandel 2006). It is similar to other commonly used concepts such as adaptability, coping ability, management capacity, stability, robustness, flexibility and resilience (Smit and Wandel 2006). Ecosystem resilience is the capacity of an ecosystem to tolerate disturbance without the system undergoing fundamental changes in its functional characteristics. A resilient ecosystem can withstand shocks and rebuild itself when necessary (Folke 2006). Gallopin (2006) notes that resilience is also a component of the capacity of a social system to respond to change. According to Folke et al. (2003), four critical factors are necessary for building resilience and adaptive capacity in social-ecological systems in the context of change. These four factors, which interact across temporal and spatial scales are: learning to live with change and uncertainty, nurturing diversity for reorganization and renewal, combining different types of knowledge for learning and creating opportunity for self-organization toward social-ecological sustainability (Folke, Colding, and Berkes 2003). In managing resilience, adaptive capacity influences a social-ecological system by modulating between maintenance of the status quo and transformation of the system to a new state, depending on which is most desirable (Engle 2011).

In the climate change literature, adaptive capacity is the ability of a system to act and adjust to climate change by changing its characteristics to moderate potential damage, but also take advantage of opportunities (Levine, Ludi, and Jones 2011). It is generally accepted as a positive attribute of a system for reducing vulnerability or fostering resilience (Engle 2011). Adaptive capacity is a vector of resources and assets that represent the base from which adaptation actions and investments can be made (Adger and Vincent 2005). Some determinants of adaptive capacity are mainly local while others reflect more general socio-economic and political systems. They include economic wealth, technology, information and skills, infrastructure, institutions, social capital and equity (Smit and Pilifosova 2001, 2003). These determinants are closely interconnected and important to consider when examining strategies to enhance the capacity of a system to adapt to climate change.

The Local Adaptive Capacity (LAC) framework was developed by the Africa Climate Change Resilience Alliance (ACCRA), an alliance, established in 2009, of five development organizations; Oxfam Great Britain, Overseas Development Institute, Save the Children, World Vision International and Care International. According to Levine et al. (2011), ACCRA was established with the aim of understanding how development interventions can contribute to adaptive capacity at the community and household level, and inform the planning of development interventions. Most frameworks to conceptualize adaptive capacity have focused on assets and capitals as indicators of the adaptive capacity at the community or household level (Levine, Ludi, and Jones 2011; Jones, Ludi, and Levine 2010). ACCRA felt that while such approaches are useful in helping to understand the resources at the disposal of a system to cope with and adapt to changing circumstances, they tend to mask the role of processes and functions in supporting adaptive capacity (Jones, Ludi, and Levine 2010). Therefore, in investigating the dimensions that are considered to contribute to adaptive capacity, it is necessary to move away from looking at what a system has that enables it to adapt, to recognizing what a system does that enables it to adapt (Dixit et al. 2012). The five distinct yet interrelated characteristics of the LAC framework are: the asset base, institutions and entitlements, knowledge and information, innovation, and flexible forward-looking decision-making (Jones, Ludi, and Levine 2010) (see Figure 2a and Table 2a). These characteristics should enhance adaptive capacity at the local level while also contributing to the overall capacity of the wider system.

Table 2a. The Local Adaptive Capacity characteristics and their features

Adaptive capacity at the local level Characteristic	Features that reflect a high adaptive capacity
Asset base	Availability of key assets that allow the system to respond to evolving circumstances.
Institutions and entitlements	Existence of an appropriate and evolving institutional environment that allows fair access and entitlement to key assets and capitals.
Knowledge and information	The system has the ability to collect, analyse and disseminate knowledge and information in support of adaptive activities.
Innovation	The system creates an enabling environment to foster innovation, experimentation and the ability to explore niche solutions in order to take advantage of new opportunities.
Flexible forward-looking decision-making and governance	The system is able to anticipate, incorporate and respond to change with regards to its governance structures and future planning.

Reproduced from Jones, Ludi, and Levine, 2010.

Figure 2a. Local Adaptive Capacity framework

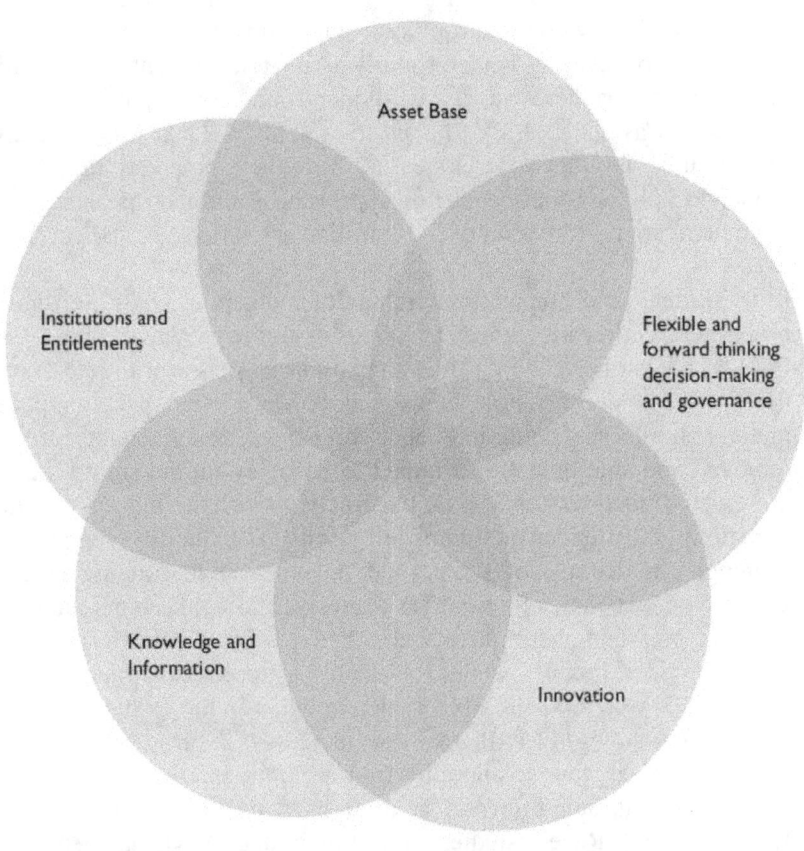

Figure reprinted with permission from Jones, Ludi, and Levine, 2010.

Farmer-Managed Natural Regeneration

Farmer-managed natural regeneration (FMNR) is a method of agroforestry in which farmers manage the naturally occurring regrowth of shoots from the stumps of trees that are present in their fields. In the 1980s, this approach was developed by Tony Rinaudo in the context of a development project in Niger in the Sahel region of Africa (Sendzimir,

Reij, and Magnuszewski 2011). According to Rinaudo (2007), the conventional approach to combat deforestation, and its consequent environmental impacts at the time, involved raising exotic tree species in nurseries and then planting, watering, protecting and weeding with ultimately little impact overall. In the midst of frustration with the vastness of the task, he recognized that what appeared to be desert shrubs were trees which were re-sprouting from stumps that were left behind in the process of clearing land for cultivation. In a moment of inspiration, he "realized that there was a vast, underground forest present all along and that it was unnecessary to plant trees at all. All that was needed was to convince farmers to change the way they prepared their fields" (Rinaudo 2007). Adoption of this approach by farmers has since led to the regeneration of trees on over 12 million acres in Niger (Bilger 2011).

In traditional land preparation, stumps of indigenous trees are removed by farmers as they are viewed as a liability to the growth of crops. Using FMNR, the farmer chooses the stumps that he or she wants to leave in the field and decides how many shoots are wanted per stump. In a method similar to pollarding and coppicing, excess shoots are then removed and side branches trimmed to half way up the stump. Farmers are given guidelines for FMNR but freely choose the number of shoots per stump, the number of stumps left per hectare, the time span between prunings and harvest of stems, and the method of pruning (Rinaudo 2007). Some stems can be cut for firewood and as the remaining stems grow in size and value each year, they protect the environment and provide fodder, humus, habitat for useful pest predators, protection from the wind, as well as shade. Experience in Niger in the 1980s showed that farmers practicing FMNR realized increases in crop yields, fodder production, fuel wood availability from pruning and thinning, as well as the potential to sell firewood in drought years (Tougiani, Guero, and Rinaudo 2009). Recent studies have shown that FMNR has been key in accelerating environmental rehabilitation; increases in numbers and diversity of trees on previously degraded land, increased soil fertility and erosion control (Larwanou and Saadou 2011).

Case Study Contexts

Ethiopia, a land-locked mountainous country, with a population of about 85 million, is the second most populous country in Sub-Saharan Africa (The World Bank 2013a). Considered to be a low income country, Ethiopia is ranked at 173 out of 187 countries in the Human Development Report 2013 with 87.3 percent of the population living in poverty. This Human Development Index is a summary measure to assess long-term progress in three basic dimensions of human development, namely a long and healthy life, access to knowledge, and a decent standard of living (United Nations Development Program 2013a). Despite continuing challenges, over the past two decades primary school enrolments have quadrupled, child mortality has been cut in half, and the number of people with access to clean water has more than doubled in the country (The World Bank 2013a).

Following the severe famine of 1984 in Ethiopia, WV, established operations in the Humbo area, located 360 km south-west of the capital city of Addis Ababa. Forests around the densely populated Humbo area were largely destroyed by the 1960s and the area experienced variable rainfall, environmental degradation, and food shortages for the 85% of the population who lived in poverty (Brown et al. 2011). While always having a focus on reforestation, WV Ethiopia began a program of community agroforestry employing natural regeneration of woody species in 2004. Besides environmental regeneration to improve livelihoods, the project also focused on carbon sequestration as a source of poverty alleviation. Seven cooperatives were established as non-profit entities and they received land-use rights. In accordance with group by-laws and constitutions, all proceeds from carbon sales will be directed to projects benefiting all community members, such as projects in education, health or agriculture (Dettman, Rinaudo, and Tofu 2008; Biryahwaho et al. 2012). In 2010, Humbo's close to 3000 hectares of regenerated forest on steep mountainside terrain became the first project in the World Bank Carbon Finance Unit's Africa portfolio to receive payments for emissions reduction (Brown et al. 2011). It is expected to sequester 880,296 tonnes of carbon dioxide equivalent (tCO2e) for an operating lifetime of 60 years with an average net anthropogenic greenhouse gas removals by sinks of 29,343.2 tCO2e per year (Biryahwaho et al. 2012).

43

More recently, the Talensi FMNR project was begun by WV Ghana and Australia, in July 2009 in the Talensi/Nabdam District, Upper East Region of Ghana, West Africa. Ghana, a middle income country, is ranked 135 out of 187 countries in the Human Development Report 2013 (United Nations Development Program 2013b). With a growing economy based on natural resources and agriculture, steady improvements are being made in life expectancy and levels of education (The World Bank 2013b). However, 31.2% of Ghana's 25 million people remain in poverty (United Nations Development Program 2013b).

Meeting with communities prior to the start of the project showed that they had witnessed widespread environmental change in their lifetimes. They reported declining crop yields, increasing insect pests, disappearance of bushlands and wildlife, more variable and severe climatic conditions and scarcity of drinking water (Rinaudo 2011). Through the WV project, 200 pilot FMNR farmers were trained and established in 10 communities. At the time of a monitoring visit in 2011, 125 hectares of FMNR pilot plots with stumps and shrubs pruned, were protected from bushfires. It should be noted that in both Ethiopia and Ghana, that FMNR is being practiced on non-agricultural communal grazing land. On these sites, increased agricultural production has mainly been in the form of increased livestock production due to an increase in fodder. Additionally, honey, wild foods and firewood are being harvested on what had previously been bare land (Ibrahim and Ward 2012).

Methodology

Using the LAC framework, the two case studies of FMNR projects from Ghana and Ethiopia were analysed against its five characteristics. WV project documents were reviewed and the LAC characteristics that are reflected in the case studies are highlighted (Ibrahim and Ward 2012). It is important to note that these projects were not originally developed using the LAC framework, as they were implemented prior to the development of the LAC. This analysis is not an evaluation of WV's programming, but was undertaken by the organization as a reflective exercise to inform development of programs, which from the outset seek to build both local adaptive capacity and contribute to child well-being (Ibrahim and Ward 2012). Children's well-being includes positive relationships, healthy individual development (involving physical and psycho-social health, cognitive, social and spiritual dimensions), and contexts where all children experience safety, social justice, and participation in civil society (World Vision International no date).

Promoting Local Adaptive Capacity

Asset Base

Assets include both tangible capitals (natural, physical and financial) as well as intangible ones, such as human or social capital (Jones, Ludi, and Levine 2010). In order for WV to gain acceptance from the local community to carry out the FMNR approach, it was important to ensure that people continued to have access to alternative natural assets to replace the ones, which they were obtaining via unsustainable methods. For example, the FMNR approach develops 'asset diversity' through encouraging the use of branches pruned from fast growing timber species for fuel wood, rather than cutting down whole trees for the production of charcoal. The communities in Ghana were also incentivised to change their behaviour through prizes offered by the local government such as donkey carts, ploughs and bicycles for the best 'environmentally friendly' community. In addition, any community which was bushfire-free for three years would be eligible for a development scheme of their choice whether it be school, water supply, electricity or health clinic. It is important to note however, that over time, the greatest incentives in both countries were the direct benefits from reforestation themselves (wood, fodder, fruits, environmental services such as reduced erosion, wind speed and temperatures, return of wildlife and recharged groundwater sources).

In both Ghana and Ethiopia the communities practising FMNR have found financial savings. In Ethiopia, increased financial assets have come to the community from the money paid for carbon credits generated under the Clean Development Mechanism (CDM). Legally recognized cooperatives in each of the seven villages adjacent to the project site make decisions regarding the use of the revenues. To maintain transparency and accountability, a series of financial safeguards were put in place to ensure that the cooperatives receive the revenues assigned to them, including external auditing of bank accounts through which the carbon revenues flow. The communities in Humbo have prioritised several areas for investment using the carbon credit revenues, including construction of a grain store and flour mill, and providing

45

micro-credit for livestock and trade. Establishment of user rights to the forest by the community means that the cooperatives are also entitled to all forest products, including timber, firewood, fodder, wild fruits, honey and indigenous medicines. Having access to these sources of natural and financial assets empowers the community to take advantage of opportunities to build their adaptive capacity, and therefore contribute to the prevention or reduction of the negative impact of shocks and stresses.

Institutions and Entitlements

Institutions are the 'rules' that govern belief systems, behaviour and organizational structure (Ostrom 2005). At the local level, these may be informal rules, such as land tenure rules, or more formal groups through which assets are shared. For FMNR approaches to be successful they depend on the support of the local community to adopt such practices. This in turn requires both appropriate institutions governing access to land and resources, and the ability to change deeply held beliefs and behaviour. To deal with some of these issues, WV set up committees and cooperatives as organisational structures to manage the FMNR project areas with technical support from local WV staff. In Ghana this involved establishing committees with equal numbers of men and women to be trained in FMNR, and then to lead other members of the community to adopt the practice. In Ethiopia, seven cooperatives were created with membership open to all interested community members.

The formation of cooperatives and committees has aided with the formalisation of land tenure agreements. The cooperatives in Ethiopia are recognised under Ethiopian law and granted land-use rights in the project areas. In Ghana where the nine communities involved are practising FMNR primarily on communal land, land use guidelines were prepared with community-based bylaws being jointly devised, which enable communities to manage the forest themselves with the support from the District Assembly. The establishment of formal land use rights has been particularly important in Ethiopia and enabled the project to be eligible for carbon credits. All the cooperatives have agreed to transfer the carbon trading rights from the cooperatives to the participating villages. This was important in terms of ownership and entitlement to resources from the project.

Innovation

Experimentation, innovation and adoption as part of the learning process are essential in ensuring the system's ability to cope with and respond to changing circumstances. However, at the local level the willingness and capacity to foster innovation vary widely (Jones, Ludi, and Levine 2010). While FMNR represented an innovative approach to land management practices in both countries, WV staff, had to overcome a dominant culture that didn't believe that such approaches would work. One of the keys to the successful uptake of innovation is understanding how to ease constraints preventing the spread of good ideas. The FMNR projects facilitated this by setting in place the appropriate institutional framework (cooperatives, land use agreements etc.) and enabling farmers to witness the benefits of such an approach through peer learning exchanges. This, combined with the trust built up by the history of the NGO in the area meant that the communities were open to try this innovative approach (Brown et al. 2011; Dettman, Rinaudo, and Tofu 2008). The fact that use of FMNR techniques shows environmental improvements in a short space of time also aided in fostering adoption of the innovations beyond the initial participants.

Flexible Forward-thinking Decision-making and Governance

In social-ecological systems, the existence of governance institutions that learn and store knowledge and experience, create flexibility in problem solving and balance power among interest groups, play an important role in enhancing adaptive capacity (Tompkins and Adger 2004; Walker et al. 2006; Pahl-Wostl 2009). WV gained the support of the local government, traditional chiefs and land custodians first, which was critical to gaining the widespread support of the community. One WV Ghana staff was quoted as saying "We realized that community structures were needed. This is a key to the success of the Talensi FMNR project – we went to the leaders and won them first. Sometimes we worked until midnight in the communities at the start." (Rinaudo 2011). Ensuring good governance and improving traditional governance structures for environmental protection has been a strong feature of the project. In Ethiopia, the success of the Humbo project has led the government to consider mainstreaming carbon finance into its sustainable land management programme as a new model of sustainability, and declare a target of replicating the FMNR model on 15 million hectares of land.

Knowledge and Information

Promoting FMNR involved informing and educating people about the impact of their current practices on the quality of the natural resources in the area, through radio messages and training sessions for the farmer committees and cooperatives. However, it was also important that people were able to perceive the changes themselves and not just be told about them. The communities had spent substantial time and money in the past on tree planting which had not delivered results. This meant that at the beginning there was a lack of belief that adopting yet another approach would work. To help combat that unbelief, WV facilitated the travel of twenty farmers from Ghana to Burkina Faso to learn from their counter-parts on re-greening initiatives. This form of 'peer-to-peer learning' was particularly effective and was instrumental to the success of the project in Talensi. According to Rinaudo (2011), meeting Yacouba Sawadogo, "the man who turned back the desert" (Dodd 2009), had a big impact on the group, so much so that one farmer aspires to be Ghana's Sawadogo. The project in Ghana also had to deal with challenging the deeply-held belief that bush fires were an inevitable occurrence during the dry season and nothing could be done to prevent them. Fire prevention training helped people to understand that this was not the case, and equipped them with the knowledge and skills to prevent the incidence and spread of fire in the future.

Both projects, in Ethiopia and Ghana, have linked farmers with agricultural extension workers, research services such as the Forest Research Institute, and Government departments such as the Natural Disaster Management Organisation, Ministry of Food and Agriculture, and the Education service. This should result in an effective flow of relevant information between local institutions and communities, ensuring that farmer committees and cooperatives are aware of potential climate impacts and can make informed decisions. The establishment of these relationships is also important in providing a two-way flow of information so that local government departments and services understand the needs of farmers and are better able to tailor their support. This is key to developing adaptive capacity and supporting appropriate adaptation strategies at the local level.

Discussion and Conclusion

The FMNR approach has resulted in increased agricultural production and income levels of farmers in both the Talensi and Humbo regions of Ghana and Ethiopia. In the Talensi region of Ghana approximately 125 hectares of marginalised and degraded lands is being restored through tree regeneration with stumps and seeds in the soil and through protection from bush fire. In Humbo in Ethiopia, the project is successfully regenerating close to 3000 hectares of land. This has resulted in better soil quality, protection of fragile water catchment areas, production of sustainable firewood and fodder, and wild fruits and wildlife becoming available again. Restoration of the natural capital in both regions increases the overall resilience of the social-ecological system as it is better able to respond to disturbance and changing circumstances (Folke 2006; Garrity et al. 2010). This in turn increases the asset base of the local communities to adapt to climate change as a result of improved sources of livelihoods. This comes not only from improvements in the diversity of agro-ecological goods and services but also in the case of Ethiopia, in the form of payments for environmental services (carbon sequestration) for the global community. Results of a study in Niger suggest that increases in crop and tree diversity associated with FMNR adoption, provide a more diverse portfolio of livelihoods, including potential for payment for environmental services, that may enable households to be better prepared to cope with the unpredictable risk of a changing climate (Haglund et al. 2011). Given WV's focus on CWB as their measure of success, these projects could contribute to improvements in children's health as a result of increased food and livelihood security. Furthermore, children would be able to spend more time in school since they would not have to walk long distances from home to find fruits and food to eat.

The case studies from Ghana and Ethiopia demonstrate that secure livelihoods and increased adaptive capacity do not only depend on the existence of increased assets alone. The recognition of appropriate rights to land, natural resources and revenues, as well as the formation of local institutions which are legally recognized and accountable to local people is crucial. Such an enabling institutional environment determines access to assets and the knowledge and understanding that people have to make decisions, use and develop the assets. The importance of supportive

49

institutional arrangements and policies was demonstrated in a study conducted by the World Agroforestry Center in three countries in the Sahel, which found that a significant barrier to adoption of FMNR was unreasonable forest codes and 'heavy-handedness' on the part of forest officers (Place and Binam 2013). Similarly, Sendzimir, Reij and Magnuszewski (2011) noted that in Niger, changes in livelihoods and the biophysical environment were preceded by institutional changes in governance. Institutions have been shown to play a key role in fostering adaptive capacity in the broader climate change and environmental governance literature (Tompkins and Adger 2004; Walker et al. 2006; Pahl-Wostl 2009).

Combining different types of knowledge for learning and creating opportunity for self-organization toward social-ecological sustainability is important for building adaptive capacity and resilience (Folke, Colding, and Berkes 2003). Exchange of such knowledge is facilitated by increased networking and connectivity between groups and stakeholders which builds adaptive capacity (Engle and Lemos 2010). The formation of networks fosters the exchange of different types of knowledge which is essential to support social learning (Pahl-Wostl 2009). The partnership of WV with communities in both areas brought new knowledge into communities. The long history of working in the Humbo area provided WV with an understanding of local needs and earned it respect as a development partner from both the community and the local government (Dettman, Rinaudo, and Tofu 2008). This trust-based, strong working relationship facilitated the successful implementation of the Humbo project. Shames et al (2012) note that international development NGOs are well placed as early actors in implementation of such projects, due to their deep experience with rural development and their longstanding local presence which lays a foundation of trust. In Ghana the opportunity that WV provided for a peer learning exchange to Burkina Faso was key in combating initial scepticism of the ability of FMNR to reverse environmental degradation. This also builds adaptive capacity as people feel confident that they are not helpless victims of climate change and desertification, but that they can do something to reverse the environmental degradation surrounding them, and create a better future for themselves and their children. As in other situations, success with FMNR will undoubtedly foster informal exchange of knowledge through local farmer's social networks (Crona et al. 2011).

50

Table 2b. Summary of indicators of adaptive capacity in two case studies.

Characteristic	Indicators of improved adaptive capacity
Asset base	➤ Restoration of forested land leading to improved environmental services, enhanced biodiversity and access to forest products. ➤ Improved livelihoods from increased agricultural production and payment for environmental services
Institutions and entitlements	➤ Recognition of rights to land, natural resources and revenues ➤ Formation of local, legally recognized institutions
Knowledge and information	➤ Partnership with WV based on an historical relationship of trust ➤ Opportunities for peer learning ➤ Formation of institutional networks
Innovation	➤ Adoption of FMNR as an innovative approach to land management ➤ Approach which overcame initial scepticism
Flexible forward-looking decision-making and governance	➤ Supportive local authorities at an early stage ➤ Ethiopian government mainstreaming carbon finance into sustainable land management programme

In conclusion, while not necessarily the goal of the projects at the outset, the introduction of FMNR appears to have been successful in fostering improved adaptive capacity and resilience in communities in Ethiopia and Ghana. This is important, as it has been shown that the impacts of climate change cannot be separated from other development pressures. Therefore, in the context of climate change, climate risks must be addressed not as a separate initiative but mainstreamed into development policy across all sectors (Levine, Ludi, and Jones 2011). In moving forward, it is important for WV to build on its success with FMNR in fostering an integrated approach to all of its development programming, by applying a resilience lens to all aspects of development, including poverty reduction, governance, conflict prevention, peace building and disaster risk reduction. Working on just on one characteristic alone, such as providing people with assets, will not lead to changes in people's capacity to anticipate, deal with and respond to adverse change. Such an integrated approach will require some changes in the organization's overall approach.

References

Adger, W. Neil, and Katharine Vincent. 2005. Uncertainty in adaptive capacity. *C.R. Geoscience* 337:399-410.

Bilger, Burkhard. 2011. The Great Oasis. *The New Yorker, December 19 & 26*, 111-121.

Biryahwaho, Byamukama, Michael Misiko, Hailu Tefera, and Assefa Tofu. 2012. Institutional innovations in African smallholder carbon projects Case Study: Humbo Ethiopia Assisted Natural Regeneration Project. CGIAR Research Program on Climate Change, Agriculture and Food Security (CCAFS).

Brown, Carolyn Peach, Douglas R. Brown, and Christopher Shore. 2014. An investigation of perception of climate change risk, environmental values and development programming in a faith-based international development organization. In *How the World's Religions are Responding to Climate Change*, edited by R. Globus Veldman, A. Szasz and R. Haluza-DeLay. New York: Routledge.

Brown, Douglas R., Paul Dettman, Tony Rinaudo, Hailu Tefera, and Assefa Tofu. 2011. Poverty alleviation and environmental restoration using the Clean Development Mechanism: A case study from Humbo, Ethiopia. *Environmental Management* 48 (2):322-333.

Crona, Beatrice, Henrik Ernstson, Christina Prell, Mark Reed, and Klaus Hubacek. 2011. Combining social network approaches with social theories to improve understanding of natural resource governance. In *Social Networks and Natural Resource Management: Uncovering the Social Fabric of Environmental Governance*, edited by O. Bodin and C. Prell. New York: Cambridge University Press.

Dettman, Paul, Tony Rinaudo, and Assefa Tofu. 2008. Case Study: The Humbo Community-based Natural Regeneration Project, Ethiopia. In *Climate Change and Forests: Emerging Policy and Market Opportunities*, edited by C. Streck, R. O'Sullivan, T. Janson-Smith and R. Tarasofsky. London: Chatham House.

Dixit, Aarjan, Heather McGray, Javier Gonzales, and Margaret Demond. 2012. The National Adaptive Capacity Framework: Assessing

Institutional Aspects of National Capacity for Climate Change Adaptation. Washington, DC: World Resources Institute.

Dodd, Mark. 2009. The Man Who Stopped the Desert. UK: 1080 Film and Television Ltd.

Eastaugh, Chris. 2010. Climate Change Impacts on African Forests and People Vienna, Austria: International Union of Forest Research Organizations.

Engle, Nathan L. 2011. Adaptive capacity and its assessment. *Global Environmental Change* 21 (2):647-656.

Engle, Nathan L, and Maria Carmen Lemos. 2010. Unpacking governance: Building adaptive capacity to climate change of river basins in Brazil. *Global Environmental Change* 20:4-13.

Folke, Carl. 2006. Resilience: The emergence of a perspective for social-ecological systems analyses. *Global Environmental Change* 16:253-267.

Folke, Carl, Johan Colding, and Fikret Berkes. 2003. Synthesis: building resilience and adaptive capacity in social-ecological systems. In *Navigating Social-Ecological Systems: Building Resilience for Complexity and Change*, edited by F. Berkes, J. Colding and C. Folke. Cambridge, UK: Cambridge University Press.

Gallopin, Gilberto C. 2006. Linkages between vulnerability, resilience, and adaptive capacity. *Global Environmental Change* 16:293-303.

Garrity, Dennis Philip, Festus K. Akinnifesi, Oluyede C. Ajayi, Sileshi G. Weldesemayat, Jeremias G. Mowo, Antoine Kalinganire, Mahamane Larwanou, and Bayala Jules. 2010. Evergreen Agriculture: A robust approach to sustainable food security in Africa. *Food Security* 2:197-214.

Haglund, Eric, Jupiter Ndjeunga, Snook Laura, and Dov Pasternak. 2011. Dry land tree management for improved household livelihoods: Farmer managed natural regeneration in Niger. *Journal of Environmental Management* 92:1696-1705.

Ibrahim, Maggie, and Nicola Ward. 2012. Promoting Local Adaptive Capacity: Experiences from Africa and Asia. Milton Keynes, UK: World Vision UK.

Jones, Lindsey, Eva Ludi, and Simon Levine. 2010. Towards a characterisation of adaptive capacity: A framework for analysing adaptive capacity at the local level. London, UK: Overseas Development Institute.

Larwanou, Mahamane, and M. Saadou. 2011. The role of human interventions in tree dynamics and environmental rehabilitation in the Sahel zone of Niger. *Journal of Arid Environments* 75:194-200.

Levine, Simon, Eva Ludi, and Lindsey Jones. 2011. Rethinking Support for Adaptive Capacity to Climate Change: The Role of Development Interventions. London, UK: Overseas Development Institute.

McGray, Heather, Anne Hammill, and Rob Bradley. 2007. Weathering the Storm: Options for Framing Adaptation and Development. Washington, DC: World Resources Institute.

Mitchell, Tom, and Thomas Tanner. 2006. Adapting to Climate Change: Challenges and Opportunities for the Development Community. Teddington: Institute of Development Studies and Tearfund.

Mitchell, Tom, and Maarten van Aalst. 2008. Convergence of Disaster Risk Reduction and Climate Change Adaptation: A Review for DFID. London: Institute of Development Studies.

Ostrom, Elinor. 2005. *Understanding Institutional Diversity*. Princeton, NJ: Princeton University Press.

Pahl-Wostl, Claudia. 2009. A conceptual framework for analysing adaptive capacity and multi-level learning processes in resource governance regimes. *Global Environmental Change* 19:354-365.

Place, Frank, and Joachim Nyemeck Binam. 2013. Economic Impacts of Farmer-Managed Natural Regeneration in the Sahel: End of Project Technical Report for Free University Amsterdam and IFAD. Nairobi: ICRAF.

Rinaudo, Tony. 2007. The development of farmer managed natural regeneration. *LEISA Magazine* 23 (2):32-34.

———. 2011. Talensi Farmer Managed Natural Regeneration (FMNR) project Monitoring Visit Report. Victoria, Australia: World Vision Australia.

Sendzimir, Jan, Chris P. Reij, and Piotr Magnuszewski. 2011. Rebuilding resilience in the Sahel: Regreening in the Maradi and Zinder regions of Niger. *Ecology and Society* 16 (3):1.

Shames, Seth, Eva Wollenberg, Louise E. Buck, Patti Kristjanson, Moses Masinga, and Byamukama Biryahwaho. 2012. Institutional innovations in African smallholder carbon projects CCAFS Report No. 8. CGIAR Research Program on Climate Change, Agriculture and Food Securtiy (CCAFS).

Smit, Barry, and Olga Pilifosova. 2001. Adaptation to climate change in the context of sustainable development and equity. In *Climate Change 2001: Impacts, Adaptation, and Vulnerability - Contribution of Working Group II to the Third Assessment*

Report of the Intergovernmental Panel on Climate Change, edited by J. J. McCarthy, O. F. Canziani, N. A. Leary, D. J. Dokken and K. S. White. Cambridge: Cambridge University Press.

————. 2003. From adaptation to adaptive capacity and vulnerability reduction. In *Climate Change, Adaptive Capacity and Development*, edited by J. Smith, R. T. J. Klein and S. Huq. London: Imperial College Press.

Smit, Barry, and Johanna Wandel. 2006. Adaptation, adaptive capacity and vulnerability. *Global Environmental Change* 16:282-292.

The World Bank. 2013. *Ethiopia Overview*. The World Bank 2013a [cited July 3 2013]. Available from http://www.worldbank.org/en/country/ethiopia/overview.

————. 2013. *Ghana Overview*. The World Bank 2013b [cited July 3 2013]. Available from http://www.worldbank.org/en/country/ghana/overview.

Tompkins, Emma L., and W. Neil Adger. 2004. Does adaptive management of natural resources enhance resilience to climate change? *Ecology and Society* 9 (2):10.

Tougiani, Abasse, Chaibou Guero, and Tony Rinaudo. 2009. Community mobilisation for improved livelihoods through tree crop management in Niger. *GeoJournal* 74:377-389.

Toulmin, Camilla. 2009. *Climate Change in Africa*. Edited by A. de Waal and R. Dowden, *African Arguments*. London: Zed Books.

United Nations Development Program. 2013a. The Rise of the South: Human Progress in a Diverse World Human Development Report 2013, Ethiopia. In *Human Development Report 2013*. New York: United Nations Development Program.

————. 2013b. The Rise of the South: Human Progress in a Diverse World Human Development Report 2013, Ghana. In *Human Development Report*. New York: United Nations Development Program.

Walker, Brian, Lance Gunderson, Ann Kinzig, Carl Folke, Steve Carpenter, and Lisen Schultz. 2006. A handful of heuristics and some propositions for understanding resilience in social-ecological systems. *Ecology and Society* 11 (1):13.

World Vision International. 2008. World Vision Overview: Hope for the Most Vulnerable. Monrovia: World Vision International.

————. 2011. *World Vision International: Climate Change Response Initiative*. World Vision International 2010 [cited 7 April 2011]. Available from

http://www.wvi.org/wvi/wviweb.nsf/maindocs/C799F54BADD
D6FA1882574BF007F82CB?opendocument.

———. 2011. Annual Review 2011. World Vision International.

———. 2013. *World Vision International: Our History* 2013 [cited July 4 2013]. Available from http://www.wvi.org/our-history.

———. no date. Child Well-Being Reference Guide. World Vision International.

Seeking explanations for the 'wind turbine syndrome' debate in Ontario, Canada: Contributions from procedural justice in the form of community power

Chris Buse[1,2,3], Cheryl Teelucksingh[4] and Rebecca Hasdell[1,2]

[1] Dalla Lana School of Public Health, University of Toronto
[2] CIHR Fellow in Public Health Policy
[3] Lupina Research Associate, Comparative Program on Health and Society
[4] Associate Professor, Department of Sociology, Ryerson University

Introduction

Wind turbines (WTs) and other renewable sources of energy are increasingly being considered by policy actors to address energy insecurity and environmental concerns such as climate change. As alternative energy generation continues to increase in North America, WTs have coincidentally emerged as a controversial topic in environmental public health. Some individuals residing near WTs have reported symptoms of nausea, anxiety, depression, insomnia, fatigue and headaches which have been dubbed 'wind turbine syndrome' (Pierpont 2009). Despite these assertions, existing expert panel reviews comprised of audiologists and medical doctors claim there is no biological link between living in close proximity to a WT and experiencing the reported symptoms (see Chief Medical Officer of Health of Ontario 2010; Colby et al. 2009). Rather, these reviews and much of the peer-review literature tend to emphasize that annoyance associated with the loss of natural aesthetics is at the core of the ill-health reports (Knopper and Ollson 2011). This chapter offers an alternative framing to this debate by emphasizing the importance of psychosocial pathways to ill-health and the role of procedural justice as it is related to WT development. Procedural justice refers to the inclusion of the public in WT decision-making related to the siting and management of wind infrastructure, and a more fulsome definition of this concept and its relationship to public participation and the energy justice literature are provided later in this chapter.

Our primary hypothesis is that in the case of WTs, a lack of procedural justice and the exclusion of communities from decision-making processes is a possible antecedent cause of psychosocial stress that may indirectly contribute to ill health claims in communities most affected by WTs. Rather than focussing solely on the biomedical dimension of WTs, this hypothesis offers a theoretical engagement with the sociopolitical drivers on the pathway between WTs and ill-health. If we are to believe that the reported ill-health effects are in part tied to the stress-inducing process of wind farm development rather than a biophysical causal mechanism, then policies and programs aiming to change the relationship between local residents and WT infrastructure, such as community power, merit more serious consideration (Buse 2012).

Building on insights from the scholarly literature on energy and procedural justice, this chapter situates community power—that is, the localization of independent energy generation and production in communities—as a novel policy and community-led response to emerging health concerns related to the development of WTs in North America. We argue that an energy justice approach to implementing WTs would advocate for more active participation of affected communities and the questioning of relations of power implicated in and reproduced through the greening of the power sector. This is especially important given that access to the power grid for more diverse players is the site where attempts to enact environmental justice principles of democratic participation has the most potential (Teelucksingh and Poland 2011).

Using the example of Ontario, Canada, we first situate the growth of wind energy generation within the historical development of Ontario's renewable energy policy landscape, highlighting the concept of community power and describing its role as a core component of Ontario's *Green Energy Act* (2009). We then outline the emerging health effects of WTs, situating these concerns in relation to scholarly work on energy and procedural justice. The chapter ends with a discussion of how community power may offer a more transparent, democratic and participatory process for developing renewable energy technologies such as WTs. We offer empirical support for the perceived benefits and potential of community power, drawing from an analysis of expert interviews with key informants in Ontario's environmental not-for-profit sector (N=8).

Energy policy, WT development and the advent of community power in Ontario

Wind energy production is increasing. Globally, wind power generation has risen by more than 20% between 2011 and 2012, with Canada adding 935MW of new wind power generation in 2012 to bring the national total to 6200MW of available power generation (GWEC 2013). While Canada ranked 6th in wind power generation in 2012 when compared with other countries around the world (CANWEA 2012), its provinces have traditionally had exclusive rights to manage and develop the generation and production of electrical energy (Government of Canada: Section 92A, *The Constitution Act* 1867). In Ontario, Canada's second largest and most populous province, over 1500MW of wind generating capacity—approximately 5.2% of the province's total energy supply—had been installed by the end of 2012, with an additional 1719MW of generating capacity scheduled to come online by 2014 (IESO 2013). According to the Centre for Energy (2013), Ontario has installed 35.7 per cent of Canada's total wind-generated electrical capacity, with the majority of these projects spatially clustered in sections of southern and eastern Ontario. Efforts to diversify Ontario's energy supply are projected to increase wind power generation to 10% of the total provincial supply mix by 2030 (Ontario Ministry of Energy 2012). The Ontario Ministry of Energy (2012) outlines the Ontario government's long term plans for renewable energy, including wind power.

The significant increase in wind generating capacity in Ontario reflects a broader change in the province's energy policy. A full review of these policy changes is beyond the scope of this chapter, and Rowlands (2007) has written at length to conceptualize the relatively stable and incremental nature of energy policy throughout the province's history. However, recent developments to renewable energy policy have altered the existing policy landscape and merit deeper discussion.

In 2009, Ontario committed to further developing and expanding the use of renewable energy by enacting the *Green Energy Act* (2009) (GEA), which was devised to build a green energy economy that protects the environment while simultaneously creating green jobs (Ontario Ministry of Energy and Infrastructure 2009). For some, the GEA is a unique form of labour-environmentalism designed to respond simultaneously to the climate change crisis and Ontario's crisis in manufacturing (Nugent 2011). Modeled after innovative renewable energy policies in Germany, France and Denmark that were developed for similar purposes, the GEA seeks to expand renewable energy capacity in Ontario through the use of solar, wind and biogas technologies to supplement existing fossil fuel and nuclear power generating plants, and to provide new opportunities for the workforce to engage in aspects of research, innovation, manufacturing and project development/management. The GEA also revised safety standards, amending the existing Ontario *Environmental Protection Act* for renewable energy technologies and implemented safe set back limits for WTs of 550m from the nearest occupied building.

The GEA divided renewable energy generation into two streams. First, it offered novel policy incentives in the form of a revised provincial feed-in tariff (FITs) program, which provided a guaranteed return on capital investments for the development of renewable energy projects and prioritization of grid connection to such projects. The second stream took the form of micro-FITs or community power (Ontario Ministry of Energy and Infrastructure 2009). FITs were intended for larger players, including foreign investors who would generate renewable energy in Ontario in exchange for access to the grid. In contrast, the community power stream enabled smaller players (for example, farmers, community-based organizations, and households), who are normally not involved in power generation to participate in energy generation via renewables, but primarily wind turbines and solar panels). The addition of community power was considered a significant addition to the GEA. It also reflects the notion that community participation in the renewable energy transition is essential (Wirth 2014).

Community power initiatives were first developed in Germany and Denmark (Toke, Breukers and Wolsink 2008). While numerous definitions and meanings of 'community-owned production and use' exist (Walker 2010), the concept of community power refers to initiatives that are invested in, developed, owned (i.e. typically 50% ownership share or greater) and operated by community members

(Ontario Ministry of Energy and Infrastructure 2009). The Ontario Sustainable Energy Association (OSEA) additionally describes community power initiatives as locally owned projects with distributed generation sourced from low-impact renewable energy, which is accessible to local members of the community, economically viable, and locally sited, developed and appropriate for that place. Community members make key decisions including what kind of project (i.e. size, scope, or scale) they want to cultivate, where it should be sited, and how it should be managed. Since residents invest directly in the project, they also reap the direct financial benefits that result from co-ownership. Community power is increasingly described in the European literature (Bergman and Eyre 2011; Devine-Wright and Devine-Wright 2009; Walker and Devine-Wright 2008; Walker, Hunter, Devine-Wright and Evans 2007; Van der Horst 2008), but has received limited mention in the Canadian context (Teelucksingh and Poland 2011).

Research on community power in Canada suggests that despite a policy landscape that supports the participation of more diverse stakeholders in power generation, the practice of renewable energy generation has privileged more powerful stakeholders, such as businesses, developers, and investors, in the form of FITs (Teelucksingh 2013). In contrast, less powerful players including farmer, churches, and schools, have been less successful with initiating community power projects due to their lack of access to start-up capital, time, expertise, and knowledge (Teelucksingh 2013). Indeed, critics of the GEA state that thus far, the regulatory licensing process is biased in favour of large power companies instead of focusing on community-led initiatives (Stevens 2009).

The emergence of 'WT syndrome' in Ontario

The introduction of the GEA and its associated FIT and microFIT programs is a key factor in the expansion of wind generating capacity in Ontario described above. In light of these developments, concerns related to living in close proximity to WTs have emerged from around the province. The opposition to the development of WTs has been primarily on the basis of health outcomes and associated decreases in property values that are allegedly linked to living near industrial WT sites (those capable of producing 50MW of electricity or more) (Krogh et al. 2011).

As described above, such production sites are often owned and operated by industrial power operators with little community control over the development or siting of these projects.

Existing set back regulations for the development of wind energy projects in Ontario were determined in accordance with comprehensive scans of the peer-review literature and in consultation with audiologists and health professionals throughout the policy process. Additionally, two systematic reviews exist outlining the physical and scientific basis for the health effects associated with human exposure to WTs. For example, the Chief Medical Officer of Health of Ontario (2010) conducted a synthesis of the literature and found that people typically report turbines as an annoyance, but that no direct causal link can explain any physical health impacts. An expert panel comprised of audiologists, medical doctors and acoustical professionals from Canada, the United States, Denmark and the United Kingdom found similar results (Colby et al. 2009), stating that the sounds emitted by WTs are not unique and that there is no evidence that the audible or sub-audible sounds emitted by WTs have any direct adverse physiological effects. Instead, these reports indicate that the 'nocebo effect'—where belief in adverse health effects manifests real health outcomes—could be playing a role particularly among those who are vehemently opposed to living in close proximity to WTs or those people not consulted in the siting of particular wind energy projects.

Internationally, communities have a variety of responses to WT development. Several countries including South Africa (Lombard and Ferriera 2014), Germany, Denmark and the UK express high levels of support for the development of wind projects (Breukers and Wolsink 2007; Wolsink 2007). However, noise concerns related to public annoyance have been documented in some jurisdictions in Sweden and the Netherlands (Pedersen 2011) and resistance to such technologies has also been documented in Australian communities (Anderson 2013).

Despite expert reviews of the scientific evidence, resistance to wind power on the basis of ill-health continues to persist, with cases of noise and health related complaints being recorded in the media, academic literature and one self-published 'academic' book (see Pierpont 2009). For example, Shepherd et al. (2011) indicate that living within two kilometres of a WT in New Zealand can significantly impact overall quality of life, physical quality of life and environmental quality of life, with persons experiencing significantly lower sleep quality, perhaps tied to less restful environmental surroundings. Further, a cross-sectional study from Ontario found that as distance from WTs increased, self-reported vertigo decreases and quality of sleep increases (Paller, Bigelow, Majowicz, Law and Christidis 2013).

However, these results are complicated by literature suggesting that expectations of health risk and associated 'injustices' from WT siting are a primary driver to WT resistance and associated health effects (Songsore and Buzelli 2014). A recent study by Chapman, St. George, Waller and Cakic (2013) conducted a historical audit of health complaints in Australia and found that geographical variations in complaints are consistent with a nocebo effect. Similarly, empirical research from New Zealand found that expectations of ill health effects of WTs can produce symptoms reported to be similar to those as wind turbine syndrome (Crichton, Dodd, Schmid, Gamble and Petrie 2013). Indeed, some studies report statistical associations between personal perceptions of WTs and annoyance (Pedersen & Waye 2007), and that a dose-response relationship was found between exposure to WTs and perceived annoyance. However, controlling for respondent's attitudes towards the visual impact of WTs on the scenery and landscape seems to explain the association between exposure and perceived annoyance (Pedersen & Waye 2004). These findings were reiterated by Knopper and Olison (2011) who additionally conclude that attitudes towards WTs and individual sensitivity to noise are of key importance in explaining reported impacts. The resulting uncertainty of ill-health claims—when weighed against the empirical literature—has led some scholars to call for decision-making principles such as the Least Impactful Means Test, the Neighbour Principle, or the Precautionary Principle to guide the ethical development of WT siting and development (Shain 2011).

In order to better understand the debates both between and within the grey and academic literatures, Canada's federal health agency, Health Canada, is presently conducting empirical research of its own to determine the health impacts of WTs on the wellbeing of Canadians. At present, such analysis has been rooted primarily in biomedical explanations of the relationship between WTs and health, perhaps over-emphasizing the relationship between exposure to the physical infrastructure of WTs and the manifestation (or not) of biophysical health impacts. In this chapter, we suggest that the discrepancy might be resolved through an analysis of the social production (i.e. the social context and political dynamics related to the placement of WTs) and the implementation of these technologies.

For example, additional empirical research has found that persons who share ownership and reap the direct financial benefits of WTs have a decreased risk of annoyance despite exposure to similar sound levels as others who live within the same proximity (Pedersen et al. 2009), and that community ownership can significantly influence public perceptions towards wind energy technologies (Warren and McFadyen 2010). Due to the perceived benefits of community power, including financial incentives for participants, it may be possible that the social process under which these technologies are developed acts as a mediating influence to ill-health, primarily on the basis of its perceived potential to involve communities directly in the process of local power generation. We therefore argue that the apparent discrepancy between heavily medicalized accounts of the biophysical connection between WT technologies and ill-health are insufficient to understanding the social processes and structural conditions involved in WT project development, implementation and operation. Whether the ill health effects are perceived or actualized, we contend that the systematic privileging of industry interests over community interests can contribute to disempowerment, marginalization, and resulting opposition to wind power.

Beyond Wind Turbine Syndrome: Energy and Procedural Justice

In an attempt to fill the space between expert and lay testimony on the health effects of WTs, some researchers have begun to comment on the loss of social justice for individuals living near wind turbines due to their lack of consultation or involvement in the planning and implementation process (Krogh 2011). Previously conducted empirical research on procedural injustice found that perceptions of injustice, unfairness, or a lack of autonomy are positively associated with self-reported ill-health (Kivimaki et al. 2007). These findings are largely in agreement with the scholarly literature documenting the importance of psychosocial pathways to ill-health which articulate the importance of social hierarchy and disempowerment in producing ill-health outcomes (see Brunner and Marmot 1999; Marmot 2003; Martikainen, Bartley and Lahelma 2002). Ensuring procedural and democratic fairness in the licensing and siting of WTs is therefore an important component part of the policy process that could reduce disempowerment experienced by residents in the immediate vicinity of WTs.

Fairness in the siting of locally undesirable land uses has a long history in the environmental and energy justice literature, where the siting of facilities that provide a public good are often met with resistance when sited in a community's backyard (Been 1993). As argued by Amerasinghe et al. (2008), procedural justice has been significant to the environmental justice movement's claims of disproportional environmental and social risks experienced by marginalized communities, since procedural justice is often a prerequisite to distributive justice in environmental decision-making.

Procedural justice is a term used in a variety of contexts, including legal and social justice arenas, to refer to fairness, transparency, and public participation in decision-making and resource allocation process (Bell and Rowe 2012). Ebreo, Linn, and Vining's (1996, p.1262) social psychological consideration of the link between procedural justice and the public support for environmental policies, identifies that conceptions of distributive justice are tied to judgements regarding the fairness of outcomes in decision-making processes. Fairness in outcome includes the specific rules that are intended to balance stakeholders' motivation to maximize their own or their groups' self- interests. Ebro et al (1996) further distinguish between two models of procedural justice. Instrumental models are procedural decisions intended to serve the interests of those persons or groups affected by the decision. In contrast, with relational models, procedural control is determined based on the social relationships between the parties, including individual or group status and values. Based on these two models, procedural justice can serve different social and political objectives as well as various conceptions of what equitable participation and decision-making might entail. Scholarly research that examines uncertainty and risk also highlights that how individuals or groups respond to variations in procedural justice are associated with the level of uncertainty or risk (De Cremer and Sedikides, 2005) or the legitimacy of the authority or institution responsible for defining the decision-making process

(Sunshine and Tyler, 2003).

Ottinger, Hargrave and Hopson (2014) outline that wind energy is largely governed by regional or national governments who have primary control over siting requirements of wind projects, but that procedural justice is a necessary requirement in siting to resolve local issues and ensure the timely development of state and corporate led projects. Participatory techniques to illicit public participation, such as focus groups and public hearings, are ways used by energy producers to ensure both the meaningful inclusion of those who will be impacted by the environmental decisions as well as the fair distribution of the benefits and costs associated with the decisions (Amerasinghe et al. 2008). Consistent with a political economy perspective, procedural justice is concerned with identifying and addressing unequal power dynamics and the need to questions normalized decision-making that continues to privilege more powerful stakeholders (i.e. governments, developers, and industry) in the energy production process at the expense of others.

As discussed above, Ontario's GEA (2009) is a policy framework that advocates for renewable energy and community power. However, there are numerous procedural processes (such as financial costs and environmental expertise) that are barriers to broad public participation in renewal energy production. In order to complete the connection process for FIT and micro-FIT programs, a number of steps have to be completed, including obtaining approval from the Ontario Power Authority, requesting requisite information from local power providers and gaining connection approval, estimating connection costs, and having the site inspected by the local power authority and the Electrical Safety Authority (Toronto Hydro 2013). Thus, navigating the bureaucratic requirements of connecting to and accessing the grid may also favour larger organizations that have the capacity and capital to engage in the development process. Together, these biases may have, in some cases, resulted in industry developers enjoying most of the incentives built into the GEEA, stifling community projects and inhibiting their access to the supply grid.

In terms of addressing procedural barriers, Cowell et al (2012) argue that larger scale energy projects should be required to contribute to community benefit funds that will support smaller scale community power projects. Thus, energy policy must be sensitive to the social dimensions of energy development, including social acceptance, by considering the potential benefits to communities impacted by wind turbines in addition to remedying any harm caused by large-scale wind power.

Similar to our argument, Cowell et al. (2012) claim that community power initiatives can remedy the drawbacks associated with larger scale energy development. However, it is important to note that such remediation makes two important assumptions. First, that there is environmental and social capacity for both the smaller scale community power and larger scale energy development within a shared spatial vicinity. Second, that in a neo-liberal political economic context, governments, such as the Ontario government, will be willing to revise energy policy to require large scale energy producers to contribute to community benefits funds and to support local community power initiatives.

In addressing both of these points, there are opportunities for industrial WT producers to support smaller projects, or provide assistance to communities neighbouring clusters of WTs. Areas where there are a higher density of turbines may lead people to be more likely to complain, especially if they were not consulted about the development of these projects. Having large power producers assist with the development of new projects, and ensuring that those projects are appropriately sited and safe, may actually bolster support for larger wind farms that operate on a long-term time horizon, so long as noise propagation is accounted for and there are not so many wind turbines that it causes problems for locals. Additionally, existing policies have also tied the province to trade agreements with multinational corporations to develop and supply wind technologies, with no fixed requirement for local labor. The procedural injustices associated with not allowing domestic workers to capitalize on provincial policies can also impact psychosocial stress associated with a lack of new opportunities for community economic development. In other words, approaching wind turbine siting from a process oriented view can have effects that 'trickle down' into various aspects of community economic development and social acceptability.

Applying the concept of procedural justice to deliberative processes around the siting of wind energy projects can not only result in increased social acceptance, but can negate the potentially damaging effects of unfairness on a community's social well-being (Gross 2007; Hindmarsh and Matthews 2008). Given the strong links between social wellness and the rich literature on psychosocial pathways to ill-health, ensuring fairness in siting undesirable land uses is a possible mechanism by which to promote the health of communities.

Community power may therefore offer solutions to health related concerns resulting from possibly unfair or unjust WT project siting and development. In Germany, residents typically own greater than 50% of the installed electrical generation for a given project. Strong public support for wind farm development exists in Germany and Denmark (Breukers and Wolsink 2007; Wolsink 2007) where there has been a history of gradualist wind power development (Valentine 2013), and both countries have a relative absence of 'WT syndrome' as it is experienced in North America. In the Netherlands, it was found that locally owned wind energy generation projects actually accelerated implementation achievements and countered some of the resistance issues tied to the acceptance of this technology (Breukers and Wolsink 2007).

It is clear that social acceptance of renewable technologies is of primary concern if the GEA is to continue to be a successful driver of the green economy and ecological stewardship. Providing communities the opportunity to harness the means of production is a promising start, but further work may be required to ensure that project development is transparent, and fairly distributed across community and commercial interests. Indeed, the emergence of multi-actor and bottom-up models of cooperative energy generation seem to signal a governance shift in climate change policy that links local activism to national policy in ways that support spaces for direct grassroots participation and development (Walker et al. 2007). While the 'community benefits' of incentivized energy production have typically been conceived by policy makers as improving the social acceptability of wind technologies, justifications for offering significant community influence over the development and operation of a project are likely to herald additional benefits beyond the long-term sustainability of WT sites (Cowell, Bristow and Munday 2011). In other words, simply offering community members reduced rates for energy may still pose significant challenges to procedural justice and community health if community members remain outside of formal decision-making processes, or find themselves in areas with a local democratic deficit (van der Horst and Toke 2010).

"Who's got the power: The energy crisis and environmental justice in Toronto": Research Design and Setting

The previous sections of this chapter outline how the uneven implementation of provisions for community power in Ontario's GEA may have—in some instances—contributed to a lack of procedural justice for communities, and that the health repercussions of WTs might be partly explained by the psychosocial stress associated with such injustice. Building off our examination of the procedural justice literature, we now discuss how community power initiatives have been received in Ontario, drawing from an analysis of in-depth interviews (N=8) with professionals in Ontario's environmental non-governmental organization (ENGO) sector.

The data is a sub-sample of 34 interviews conducted in 2011 as a part of a SSHRC-funded study titled "Who's got the power: The energy crisis and environmental justice in Toronto". The original study was designed to examine how equity and environmental justice are being taken up by the ENGO sector in Toronto, seeking to specifically uncover personal and organizational histories as they relate to existing strengths and perceived challenges of working on energy-related issues in the Ontario context (Teelucksingh 2012). Toronto was the location for the study due to its relatively high concentration of ENGOs. Additionally, Toronto is typically seen as an energy user rather than a site for energy production and storage, despite increasing population and the recent provincial policy directive to diversify energy production in the face of increasing energy demand. In the original research project, our primary interests were to document and describe energy-related programming, policy development and partnerships, with an emphasis on those organizations addressing procedural justice issues within a broader environmental justice framing, and working to improve community development through the implementation of renewable energy projects. Interview transcripts were imported into a qualitative data management software package, and analyzed to generate and interpret emerging themes.

In the section below, we summarize the themes from the Toronto ENGO interviews with a focus on Ontario energy professionals' assessment of the link between procedural justice and community power. Interview participants were able to comment on the development of Ontario's renewable energy infrastructure, but more specifically, could also addresses the potential of community power as it currently exists in the GEA policy framework.

Interview Findings

a) **Procedural (in)justice and the GEEA**

Our interview participants were uniquely situated to discuss community power in relation to the broader policy changes that occurred throughout the province. To that end, we indicate two themes that comment on how procedural injustice is playing a role in the development of renewable energy projects around the province of Ontario. First, ENGO and energy professionals had concerns that existing grid capacity was already spoken for and promised to larger power providers, thereby inhibiting the ability of smaller energy producers to access the grid:

> "So, I'd say there's not a lot of grid left for too many new developers. So now it's a question of how you share those, you know whether or not, so there are four or five coops who will be doing public offerings this summer for projects that they have developed themselves and I'm hoping that in showing that, hey, we can raise 5 million in community capital, and we're, we did the development, we raised the investment dollars, we're now managing these investors, that that will provide a really interesting scenario for these companies to say 'wow, they can help us with their projects because they can bring capital to the

table and hopefully community buy in at the same time" (Respondent 20).

There is therefore some cause for concern over what implications this might have for prioritizing small-scale energy projects and for communities to meet their own energy needs.

Second, while ENGO and energy professionals were eager to highlight the benefits of improving participation in energy decision-making processes approach enshrined in provincial policy, they also re-emphasized concerns with the way the policy was unfolding across the province, as indicated by Stevens (2009). Some respondents indicated that existing commercial operators already have the capacity and resources to reap the greatest rewards from the existing feed-in tariff model:

"In some cases I, we, you know, the commercial side of the business can get in there, is in some ways getting in their first. They have money to build projects, and they have organization, and they have this capacity, and so they can get in a community and buy up, in some cases they're buying up the best rooftops for example. And getting access to the best land. And they're getting access to transmission, which is actually becoming a huge commodity, the ability to actually put electricity on the grid is a problem" (Respondent 13).

This is further complicated by the fact that commercial operators were already better situated than grassroots cooperatives—in terms of a working knowledge of the industry and practical expertise—to gain priority access to the grid and to develop feed-in-tariff projects once the GEA was enacted:

"So, you know, again, prime movers. The first movers were the enterprising ones within the formal Ontario Hydro that knew about hydro development or wind development, whatever development. These guys, in the mass exodus that happened in Ontario Hydro when it deregulated, and the ones who were enterprising, the first

71

movers that created these companies were the ones first on the ground and first one to the line. So, the way it worked was that they did it by what they call, what was that called again, in the queue, if you're in the queue or not" (Respondent C).

Both of these issues additionally translate into the difficulties that community operators are having in dealing with the bureaucratic siting requirements of municipalities and the power that has been granted to commercial operators. Despite the GEA's intended purpose of streamlining the development of new projects, it seems that tensions exist between developers, community members, and elected officials running particular municipalities:

"Yeah, there's always been a lot of difficulty in planning, because some municipalities have zoning rules that are quite complicated, just some municipalities have made that easier than others. The Green Energy Act was designed to streamline a lot of that red tape, and I think that's one of the areas where there's opposition. I find it really interesting, a lot of the opposition groups to the Green Energy Act don't know about all of the things I just told you about, about community engagement and opportunity, and they're really worried about the fact that local municipalities aren't able to officially intervene when it comes to siting a renewable energy project... Because the act says municipalities themselves don't have the ability to influence projects, which is actually the case in a lot more than just energy. So a lot of people are very upset about that aspect. It does mandate that local communities are consulted and there's a consultation process. That's probably an area of improvement for the act. Find ways to improve the consultation between communities and projects because I think there's a lot of tension there... There's a lot of NIMBYism and there's a lot of community groups saying 'screw you, no you can't build here.' And you know, that could definitely get incited if you also were to download the permitting down to the municipalities, right, because then you've got the municipalities putting pressure on the developers. So if that had happened, if the municipalities, so you could go to the municipalities and say the compromise for the developer is community power and push for that....And it's taken us a decade to get the FIT and you know and get things where they're at now" (Respondent 20).

However, it is important to note that in spite of the jurisdictional issues related to the process of getting community approval for a project, Respondent 20 also signals that community power might offer a unique compromise between developers and municipalities.

b) Exploring the procedural aspects of community power in Ontario's renewable energy landscape

The comments on how the GEA has unfolded in relation to community power in Ontario are useful to set the context for the perceived potential of community power. In general, the interviews highlighted five key findings related to the potential of community power to ameliorate procedural injustices. First, ENGO and energy professionals indicated that community power is beneficial for improving the economic outlook of a given community. Additional benefits of the GEA were identified as being related to unique income generation for different communities and the empowering effects that those opportunities provide:

"The community participation aspect of it is unique and a huge opportunity, for large projects, community groups can own them, aboriginal communities are developing their own projects, municipalities are getting on board...I think it was an intentional strategy because green energy is not strictly, it's an environmental thing, but it's not strictly beneficial on an environmental level. And good policy on renewable energy is very, very good from a jobs perspective, it's very very good in terms of community and farm income opportunity, we have aboriginal groups as well participating. And there's different, totally different benefits for each of those groups and it makes a lot of sense if you want to create what we view is a good policy, good policy is something that works for everybody as best as you can do that." (Respondent 13)

"So communities trying to... and a lot of localized work going on where communities are recognizing for themselves 'This [community power] is what we need to do, we need to be self-sufficient, we need to increase our own capacity to be successful and take control of some of the things that we haven't had control over' so food and energy in those ways. So those things are really, really good." (Respondent 6)

A second finding links community economic development from local energy initiatives with the benefits of direct participation in these projects to produce more a more democratic engagement with the public:

"And, you know, other things like community power is another piece of that that's in the legislation that communities can own WTs and solar panels or what have you and generate their own electricity. I mean, it goes to the grid, but individuals can do that, too. So that's really cool about it, that the average person can get involved in the generation of electricity and, you know, that's another great piece of that." (Respondent 12)

Indeed, all interview participants shared similar attitudes regarding the possibility of the GEA in prioritizing the development of renewable energy systems across the province and the resulting implications for job creation and increased community participation in decision-making processes.

However, our third finding was that the largest challenges facing community power cooperatives as identified by interview participants is finding funding to cover start-up costs. This is an especially problematic issue for community members with little economic means—relative to larger commercial operators—who are looking to open up equitable spaces for participation in power generation through investment in community power projects to gain access to feed-in tariff rates across the province:

74

"The biggest barrier to this, if you, with the FIT program you can do all the technical stuff, and once you've said I've got a project that will work and the economics of it will work out it comes down to 'great, I have a project it's awesome all we need is 3 million dollars ... right now.' And that's a barrier that's really difficult to overcome" (Respondent 20).

"And then that -- you know, if there's additional monies above, up and above the study money you've spent already, how much more do you need? And the debt financing, you know, is the debt shared, is it split and, you know, you get all into these, you know, construction general manager or general contracting risk management stuff. So, that whole development cycle, especially the front end, it was the key piece for understanding the energy sector, in regards to whether it was biomass or solar or wind or hydro. It was very critical for communities to -- for that front-end piece and it was there that they realized that they had no money, right?" (Interview C).

Yet in spite of these challenges, broad based community participation in alternative energy production is viewed as a key to the successful development of projects and their integration into community life. Interview participants therefore highlighted a fourth key finding related to the potential of community power to overcome procedural issues of participating in the direct financing of these projects. Respondent 20 indicates the significance of co-op structures as a mechanism associated with community power initiatives to open spaces for small scale participation in raising the necessary funds to implement a community power project:

"They're also trying to encourage very strongly, uh, developing co-ops. So that's the ideal form of participation if you can get it is a co-op structure that allows ordinary citizens in a community to buy very small shares to help support the project. And also the community project all the revenue generated will go back towards the community group... So you weren't just a handful of people and you were high net worth, it was much more, you know, equitable and open to any resident of Ontario to participate in. So the Trek Windshare turbine, for example, you could buy in at $100 a share, so it's open to anybody, so it's an investment opportunity or an ownership opportunity that's open to pretty much anybody to participate in until such time that you've maxed out on your requirements and you close the offering. So it's more, um, group based models of average citizens being able to participate in the ownership of renewable energy projects through their co-op or a non-profit or a charity... So it was no longer small change, for me it represented huge change that could happen, and you know that the community could actually own it, like, to me I was just floored by the whole concept, and how truly transformative it could be" (Respondent 20)

Ontario's ENGO and energy professionals emphasized that most existing community power projects are structured as co-ops to allow individuals in communities to buy small shares in the project, with members collectively make the decisions in a democratic manner. While income generation and economic development may provide unique health-enhancing benefits for communities as a whole, the importance of participatory and democratic processes was seen by interview participants as the central policy change relating to community power as described in the GEA. Expanding or diversifying participation in the energy industry is viewed by most participants as a transformative activity that holds the potential to change attitudes towards renewable energies and empower communities to self-determine and control their local economic and energy futures

However, there are still gaps to be addressed in our understanding of how community power initiatives are unfolding across the province, and the final finding from our analysis of interviews raised concerns from ENGO and energy professionals who made a point to emphasize who is *not* generating community power in Toronto and Ontario:

"There is a bit of a blind spot there in terms of marginalized communities having access…it would be interesting to see if any social housing agencies in the city are able to participate and to find a way of using their property to income generate for housing, subsidized housing" (Respondent 12).

This concern about the lack of equitable participation was echoed by another interviewee who commented on the way that microFIT projects are being taken up around the province:

"The whole environmental movement is still predominantly white and middle-class, you know, WASP type of Anglo Saxon based type people. So I don't see a lot of diversity coming into the grant program or, you know, the communities that are initiating renewable energy projects" (Respondent 20).

Thus, additional capacity building may be required to ensure that equitable participation local energy generation is available across different cross-sections of Ontario's population according to income, education, class and race/ethnicity. Additional policy research may be required to further investigate alternative policy formulations that can better address the exclusion or lack of participation in local energy generation by some groups throughout the province.

Discussion

In summary, our findings indicate the perceived emancipatory potential of community power in that it allows for greater public participation in decision-making processes around the provision and ownership of collective goods, thereby enhancing community empowerment and promoting procedural justice. While there may be cases where communities are excluded from the decision-making process around WT development, community consultation processes are built into the existing GEA legislation. However, by privileging powerful corporate actors in the development of renewable energy technologies without transferring any of the immediate benefits of hosting a potentially undesirable land use in a community, the existing legislation may in fact disempower communities from broader participation processes of energy generation. Despite concerns raised by Ontario's ENGO community about the ability for these projects to gain access to the grid in relation to larger, more powerful players in the energy sector, community power initiatives offer innovative pathways to enhance participation in energy development, and hold the potential to change public perceptions of renewable energy technologies such as WTs through unique income generating opportunities. The participatory nature of community power developments can therefore redress existing concerns about the loss of procedural justice when siting commercial wind facilities (Cowell 2012).

What is clear from our findings is that the capacity building for community power—due in large part to the efforts of Ontario's ENGO sector—is already well underway throughout the province and includes a variety of education activities around the application process and how to access start-up funds, among other important technical information related to land siting and engineering. Our findings provide insight into the feasibility of expanding community power initiatives around the province given the perceived opportunities that participatory energy generation seems to offer for communities seeking to engage in more resilient local energy security planning and development that is attentive to procedural justice.

However, as indicated by our interviewees, access to transmission continues to be an issue for small-scale energy producers, and despite supportive provincial policies to enable more equitable participation in local energy generation, and the direct participation of diverse players in Ontario's energy sector has not achieved its full potential, especially given the relatively large initial investment required to build renewable energy projects. These two emergent properties of the GEA provide examples of procedural injustice, which is further complicated by the interaction between these small-scale projects and the larger neo-liberal social and political order that allows opportunities to participate in local energy generation for some groups more than others.

In Songsore and Buzzelli's (2014) review of media discourses related to the health effects of WTs in Ontario, they caution that health concerns fuel resistance to WT technology. They also conclude that while financial incentives might promote the 'pragmatic acceptance' of WTs, that this may "result in communities silently enduring health risks to their psychological and physiological detriment" (Songsore and Buzzelli 2014, p. 292). We agree that financial incentives have been proven to promote acceptance of particular renewable energy technologies, but by attending to the social process under which such projects are developed—including community consultation on project management, and financing—our argument calls for closer attention to the social processes under which WTs are sited, developed and operated. If indeed it is the perception of health risks rather than objective risks as is proposed by the Chief Medical Officer of Health of Ontario (2010), then the process of WT development merits closer consideration.

We are mindful that the primary hypothesis of this paper—that it is the process of WT development and implementation that is linked to the ill-health accounts recorded in Ontario rather than the physical infrastructure itself—cannot be answered solely by speaking with ENGO leaders in Toronto, and that this work needs further validation through the use of additional research directly comparing the health of community power owners/operators and those communities living near industrial WT sites. Nonetheless, the transformative potential of renewable energies and community power should not be downplayed (Cowell, Bristow and Munday 2011), especially given the supportive narratives we received from ENGO practitioners actively engaged in building Ontario's renewable energy infrastructure. Our findings show that by owning the means of energy production, communities can become power producers, thereby shifting the existing discourse away from 'community vs. power producers' on the basis of an alleged biophysical connection between WT technologies and ill-health manifestations, to 'communities as power producers'. This necessarily forces those interested in the 'wind turbine syndrome debate' to critically examine the *process* by which these technologies are sited, developed, implemented and operated, in addition to the existing body of evidence on the acoustical impacts of WTs on human health.

Conclusion

Wind power—as a form of renewable energy—offers promising solutions to energy security issues and climate change while simultaneously bolstering the green economy in Ontario. Despite this, concerns around cost effectiveness, wind variability, audio-aesthetics, transparency, procedural justice and health and safety continue to mire wind power in controversy (Heagle & Pope 2011). Of these concerns, the health impacts of WTs has become especially polarizing and has drawn the most attention to those opposing such development. Considering procedural justice in the Ontario 'wind turbine syndrome' debate allowed us to theorize that community power projects can offer an alternative discourse around WTs by changing the power dynamic of community *versus* wind developer, to community *as* wind developer. By emphasizing the importance of procedural justice in the conversation around wind power development, we signal the importance of innovative policy solutions to emerging health concerns associated with the development and expansion of renewable energy technologies, such as community power.

Despite obvious challenges regarding existing relations of power determining the hierarchical distribution of projects and grid access across the province, our respondents indicated the merits of investing in community power initiatives. Not only do these co-operative models present unique income generation opportunities, but they hold the

80

potential to transform personal attitudes towards wind turbines, reduce perceived annoyance, and potentially ameliorate the disempowering results of policies that promote an uneven playing field for community actors relative to corporate interests.

In light of the challenges and strengths associated with the existing community power landscape in Ontario, there are some promising areas of research to be explored. While additional research into the impact of psychosocial pathways to stress associated with WT siting would be useful, more capacity is required to strengthen the knowledge mobilization capabilities of ENGOs who can work with lower income and marginalized community power stakeholders to become players in the emerging alternative energy sector, although this does not mean there will be any less dependency on key energy players who control grid connection. Thus, policy-oriented research may further interrogate the possibility of instituting guaranteed grid connections for micro projects that help build resilient local energy supplies. Finally, additional provincial financial support may be required to further develop community power initiatives to promote local energy security, especially in those communities with no local energy distribution company (Stevens 2009). These actions will undoubtedly contribute to mitigating climate change through emissions reductions while opening new spaces for participation in ways that promote green jobs and sustainable community economic development.

Acknowledgements

The authors would like to acknowledge Blake Poland and Sarah Wakefield for their conceptual contributions to the "Who's got the power? Energy justice in Toronto, ON" study. The authors also wish to acknowledge the time, efforts, and contributions provided by ENGO study participants, and for the feedback of three anonymous reviewers. Funding for the study was provided by the Social Sciences and Humanities Research Council of Canada.

References

Amerasinghe, Manjula, Leanne Farrell, SheeShee Jin, Nah-yoon Shin and Kristen Stelljes. 2008. *Enabling Environmental Justice: Assessment of Participatory Tools*. Background report prepared for the Environmental Department, United Nations Institute for Training and Research. Available: http://web.mit.edu/jcarmin/www/carmin/EnablingEJ.pdf [Accessed July 8, 2013]

Anderson, Carmel. 2013. "The networked minority: How a small group prevailed in a local windfarm conflict." *Energy Policy,* Accessed June 1, 2013. *http://dx.doi.org/10.1016/j.enpol.2013.02.048.*

Been, Vicki. 1993. "What's fairness got to do with it? Environmental justice and the siting of locally undesirable land uses." *Cornell Law Review* 78: 1001-1085.

Bell, Derek. and Frances Rowe. 2012. *Are climate policies fairly made?* Joseph Rowntree Foundation: York, UK.

Bell, Derek, Time Gray and Claire Haggett. 2005. "The 'social gap' in wind farm siting decisions: Explanations and policy responses." *Environmental Politics* 14(4): 460-477.

Bergman, Noam and Nick Eyre. 2011. "What role for micro-generation in a shift to a low carbon domestic energy sector in the UK?" *Energy Efficiency* 4(3): 335-353.

Breukers, Sylvia and Maarten Wolsink 2007. "Wind power implementation in changing institutional landscapes: An international comparison." *Energy Policy* 35: 2737-2750.

Brunner, Eric. and Michael Marmot. 1999. "Social organization, stress, and health." In *Social Determinants of Health,* edited by M. Marmot and R.G. Wilkinson. Oxford: Oxford University Press.

Bullard, Robert D. and Glenn S. Johnson. 2000. "Environmental justice: Grassroots activism and its impact on public policy decision making". *Journal of Social Issues* 56(3): 555-578.

Buse, Christopher. 2012. "Can community power treat 'wind turbine syndrome'?" Paper presented at ESAC 2012 Annual Meeting: Environmental Knowledge, People and Places, Waterloo, ON, June 1, 2012.

Center for Energy. 2013. "Energy by the numbers: Ontario, Canada".
    Available:
    http://www.centreforenergy.com/Documents/AboutEnergy/ByTh
    eNumbers/ONT-bythenumbers.pdf [Accessed July 1, 2013].

Chapman, Simon, Alexis St. George, Karen Waller, Vince Cakic. 2013.
    The pattern of complaints about Australian wind farms does not
    match the establishment and distribution of turbines: Support for
    the psychogenic, 'Communicated Disease' Hypothesis. *PLoS
    ONE 8(10)*: e76584. doi:10.1371/journal.pone.0076584.

Chief Medical Officer of Health of Ontario. 2010. *The Potential Health
    Impacts of wind turbines*, Toronto, ON: Queen's Printer for
    Ontario.   Available:
    http://www.health.gov.on.ca/en/public/publications/ministry_rep
    orts/wind_turbine/wind_turbine.pdf [Accessed Dec 17, 2011].

Colby, W. David, Robert Dobie, Geoff Leventhall, David M. Lipscomb
    et al. 2010. *Wind Turbine Sound and Health Effects: An Expert
    Panel   Review*,   Available:
    http://www.canwea.ca/pdf/talkwind/Wind_Turbine_Sound_and_
    Health_Effects.pdf [Accessed Dec 20, 2011]

Cowell, Rrichard, Gill Bristow and Max Munday. 2012 "Wind Energy
    and Justice for Disadvantaged Communities." Joseph Roundtree
    Foundation,   York,   UK.   Available:
    http://www.communityenergyscotland.org.uk/assets/0000/6655/J
    RF_Paper.pdf [Accessed Dec 20, 2013]

Cowell, Richard, Gill Bristow and Max Munday. 2011. "Acceptance,
    acceptability and environmental justice: The role of community
    benefits in wind energy development." *Journal of Environmental
    Planning and Management* 54(4): 539-557.

Crichton, Fiona, George Dodd, Gian Schmid, Greg Gamble, and Keith J.
    Petrie. 2013. "Can expectations produce symptoms from
    infrasound associated with wind turbines?" *Health Psychology
    33*(4): 360-364.

De Cremer, David and Constantine Sedikides. 2005. "Self-uncertainty
    and Responsiveness to Procedural Justice." *Journal of
    Experimental Social Psychology* 41(2): 157-173.

Devine-Wright, Patrick and Hannah Devine-Wright. 2009. "Public
    engagement with community-based energy service provision: An
    exploratory case study." *Energy and Environment* 20(3): 303-

317.

Ebreo, Angela, Nancy Linn, and Joanne Vining. 1996. "The Impact of Procedural Justice on Opinions of Public Policy: Solid Waste Management as an Example." *Journal of Applied Social Psychology* 26(14): 1259-1285.

Gross, Catherine. 2007. "Community perspectives of wind energy in Australia: The application of a justice and community fairness framework to increase social acceptance." *Energy Policy* 35: 2727-2736.

Hindmarsh, Richard and Catherine Matthews. 2008. "Deliberative speak at the turbine face: Community engagement, wind farms, and renewable energy transitions, in Australia." *Journal of Environmental Policy and Planning* 10(3): 217-232.

Kivimaki, Mika, Jussi Vahtera, Marko Elovainio, Marianna Virtanen, and Johannes Siegrist. 2007. "Effort-reward imbalance, procedural injustice and relational injustice as psychosocial predictors of health: Complementary or redundant models?" *Occupational and Environmental Medicine* 64(10): 659-665.

Knopper, Loren D. and Christopher A. Ollson. 2011. "Health effects and wind turbiness: A review of the literature." *Environmental Health* 10(78): 10pp.

Krogh, Carmen .M.E. 2011. "Industrial WT development and loss of social justice?" *Bulletin of Science, Technology and Society* 31(4): 321-333.

Krogh, Carmen .M.E., Lorrie, Gillis, Nicholas Kouwe and Jeff Aramini. 2011. "WindVOiCe, a self-reporting survey: Adverse health effects, industrial WTs and the need for vigilance monitoring." *Bulletin of Science Technology and Society* 31: 334-345.

Lombard, Andrea and Sanette Ferreira. 2014. Residents' attitudes to proposed wind farms in the West Coast region of South Africa: A social perspective from the South. *Energy Policy 66*: 390-399.

Marmot, Michael G. 2003. "Understanding social inequalities in health." *Perspectives in Biology and Medicine* 46(3): S9-S23.

Martikainen, Pekka, Mel Bartley and Eoro Lahelma. 2002. "Psychosocial determinants of health in social epidemiology." *International Journal of Epidemiology* 31: 1091-1093.

Martinez-Alier, Joan. 2003. "Scale, environmental justice, and unsustainable cities." *Capitalism, Nature, Socialism* 14(4): 43-62.

Ontario Ministry of Energy. 2012. *Ontario's Long-term Energy Plan: Building our Clean Energy Future.* Available: http://www.energy.gov.on.ca/docs/en/MEI_LTEP_en.pdf [Accessed July 1, 2013].

Ottinger, Gwen, Timothy J. Hargrave, and Eric Hopson. 2014. "Procedural justice in wind facility siting: Recommendations for state-led siting processes. *Energy Policy 65*: 662-669.

Paller, Claire, Phil Bigelow, Shannon Majowicz, Jane Law and Tanya Christidis. 2013. "Wind turbine noise, sleep quality, and symptoms of inner ear problems". Poster presentation at *Symposium on Sustainability,* York University, Toronto ON, October 17, 2013. Available: http://www.windaction.org/posts/38916-wind-turbine-noise-sleep-quality-and-symptoms-of-inner-ear-problems-findings#.U49s0fldWSo [Accessed April 10, 2014].

Pedersen, Eja. 2011. "Health aspects associated with WT noise—Results from three field studies." *Noise Control Engineering Journal* 59(1): 47-53.

Pedersen, Eja, Frits van den Berg, Roel Bakker, and Jelte Bouma. 2009. "Response to noise from modern wind farms in the Netherlands." *Acoustical Society of America* 126(2): 634-643.

Pierpont, Nina. 2009. *WT Syndrome.* Santa Fe, NM: K-Selected Books.

Shain, Martin. 2011. "Public health ethics, legitimacy, and the challenges of industrial wind turbines: The case of Ontario, Canada". *Bulletin of Science, Technology and Society 31*: 346.

Shepherd, Daniel, David McBride, David Welch, Kim N. Dirks and Erin M. Hill. 2011. "Evaluating the impact of wind turbine noise on health-related quality of life." *Noise and Health* 13(54): 333-339.

Songsore, Emmanuel and Michael Buzzelli. 2014. "Social responses to wind energy development in Ontario: The influence of health risk perceptions and associated concerns." *Energy Policy 69*: 285-296.

Stevens, Kristopher. 2009. "Feed-in tariffs not a good fit for everyone". Letter written to the Ministry of Energy and Infrastructure, October 15, 2009. Available: http://www.ontario-sea.org/Page.asp?PageID=122&ContentID=2215 [Accessed

April 10, 2013].

Sunshine, Jason and Tom R. Tyler. 2003. "The Role of Procedural Justice and Legitimacy in Shaping Public Support for Policing." *Law & Society Review* 37(3): 513-547.

Teelucksingh, Cheryl. 2013. "Democratizing Power: Environmental Justice in Toronto". Paper presented at *Grabbing Green Conference,* Toronto, ON, May 19, 2013.

Teelucksingh, Cheryl. 2011. "The Community Power Sector and Environmental Justice in Ontario (Canada)." Paper presented at the 10th Global Conference, Environmental Justice and Global Citizenship. Oxford University, UK, July 9, 2011. http://www.inter-disciplinary.net/wp-content/uploads/2011/06/cherylepaper.pdf

Teelucksingh, Cheryl and Blake Poland. 2011. "Energy solutions, neo-liberalism, and social diversity in Toronto, Canada." *International Journal of Environmental Research and Public Health* 8: 185-202.

Toke, David, Sylvia Breukers, and Maarten Wolsink. 2008. "Wind power deployment outcomes: How can we account for the differences?" *Renewable and Sustainable Energy Reviews* 12: 1129-1147.

Toronto Hydro. 2013. "MicroFIT connection process." Available: http://www.torontohydro.com/sites/electricsystem/electricitycons ervation/feedintariff/Pages/MicroFITConnectionProcess.aspx [accessed July 20, 2013].

Valentine, Scott V. 2013. "Gradualist best practice in wind power policy". *Energy for Sustainable Development, in press,* http://dx.doi.org/10.1016/j.esd.2013.11.003.

van der Horst, Dan. 2008. "Social enterprise and renewable energy: Emerging initiatives and communities of practice." *Social Enterprise Journal* 4(3): 171-185.

van der Horst, Dan. and David Toke. 2010. "Exploring the landscape of wind farm developments; local area characteristics and planning process outcomes in rural England." *Land Use Policy* 27: 214-221.

Walker, Gordon. 2010. "Environmental justice, impact assessment and the politics of knowledge: The implications of assessing the social distribution of environmental outcomes." *Environmental Impact Assessment Review* 30: 312-318.

Walker, Gordon. 2008. "What are the barriers and incentives for community-owned means of energy production and use?" *Energy Policy* 36: 4401-4405.

Walker, Gordon and Patrick Devine-Wright. 2008. "Community renewable energy: What should it mean?" *Energy Policy* 36(2): 497-500.

Walker, Gordan,. Sue Hunter, Patrick Devine-Wright, Bob Evans and Helen Fay. 2007. "Harnessing community energies: Explaining community based localism in renewable energy policy in the UK." *Global Environmental Politics* 7(2): 64-82.

Warren, Charles R., and Malcolm McFayden. 2010. "Does community ownership affect public attitudes to wind energy? A case study from south-west Scotland." *Land Use Policy* 27: 204-213.

Wirth, Steffan. 2014. Communities matter: Institutional preconditions for community renewable energy. *Energy Policy* 70: 236-246.

Wolsink, Maarten. 2007. "Wind power implementation: The nature of public attitudes: Equity and fairness instead of 'backyard motives'." *Renewable and Sustainable Energy Reviews* 11: 1188-1207.

Technological Tide: The Social Dynamics of Rising and Falling Interest in Geoengineering

Dr. Gary Bowden
Sociology, University of New Brunswick
glb@unb.ca

Introduction

Climate change possesses several features which separate it from the majority of environmental problems and, as a result, it is widely recognized as one of the most significant and complex of such problems. First, the diversity of processes responsible for global climate and the complexity of their interaction means there is more uncertainty about the science, even with the massive investments of research dollars that have occurred over the past decades, than is the case for similarly studied problems. Second, the scale of the problem requires institutional innovation in order to implement successful mitigation policies. Where most developed countries have institutional mechanisms that do a reasonable job of addressing local, regional and national scale environmental problems, climate change requires a global response and, hence, the creation of a policy vehicle capable of facilitating global cooperation (Haluza-Delay and Davidson, 2008). Thus, aside from the significance of climate change as a problem with implications for the fate of the planet, it also provides a strategic research site for examining the relationship between uncertainty and social innovation.

Broadly speaking, as shown diagrammatically in Figure 4a, the climate problem has three distinct phases, which define three different approaches for dealing with the problem. The horizontal arrows along the top row capture the causal relations in the anthropogenic component of climate change: human actions that alter the carbon cycle on the planetary level (e.g., fossil fuel based economies) affect the climate system leading to changes in climate that affect human welfare (e.g., altered patterns of temperature and precipitation, new diseases, etc.) and, hence, require adaptation. Each phase of the problem has an associated mode of intervention, i.e., a strategy for addressing the relevant phase. Human actions that change the climate are addressed through strategies aimed at mitigating the actions responsible for the problem. The Kyoto Protocol, for example, represents an attempt to alter global behaviour in a way that mitigates the climate problem by reducing the amount of carbon released into the atmosphere. At the other extreme, adaptation (e.g., building sea walls to protect cities from rising sea levels) is the mode of intervention available for coping with the consequences of climate change and their impact on humanity. Geoengineering, defined by the National Academy of Science (1992: 433) as "options that would involve large-scale engineering of our environment in order to combat or counteract the effects of changes in atmospheric chemistry," involves intentional efforts to manipulate the climate system. Thus, in contrast to mitigation, which involves intentional manipulation of human action in order to minimize the unintentional impacts of human actions on the climate system, geoengineering involves strategies aimed at managing the climate system itself. Stated another way, addressing the problem via either adaptation or mitigation requires large elements of social innovation while addressing the problem via geoengineering depends primarily on scientific and technological innovation.

Figure 4a. A Three-Part Definition of the Climate Problem

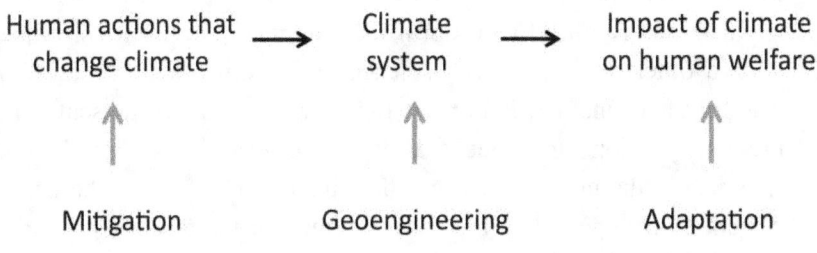

Reproduced from Keith (2000).

The current chapter documents a recent and dramatic increase in the level of attention given to geoengineering as an appropriate mode of intervention and explores the reasons behind the shift away from mitigation and toward geoengineering. Specifically, it will be argued that the emergent fascination with geoengineering is, in part, a product of climate policy politics, i.e., the failure to develop the mechanisms of international cooperation necessary for a political solution to the climate problem. In other words, the seemingly intractable issues involved in social innovations necessary to get a global policy mechanism have led to an enhanced emphasis on a scientific/technological solution that, at least at first blush, appears to avoid these problems.

This argument is developed in five parts. The first section overviews the types of geoengineering proposals and documents the trajectory of scientific and political discussion about those ideas. That trajectory, which shows the ideas have been around for a long time but have not been seriously considered until recently, raises an obvious question: what factors account for the recent rise in interest in geoengineering? The second section examines the wide variety of scientific and ethical critiques which initially marginalized geoengineering from major policy discussions. It will be shown that these issues still plague current geoengineering proposals and, hence, current interest in the approach cannot be traced to developments which did away with the previous objections. If developments in geoengineering itself are insufficient to account for the current interest, we must look elsewhere for an explanation. The third and fourth sections trace the historical trajectory of two other realms: climate science and international climate policy. The fifth and final section brings together the evidence presented in the previous sections to argue that it is changes in the social context, specifically the understanding of the climate problem and the nature of current climate policy politics, that account for the recent rise of interest in geoengineering. The chapter concludes with a discussion of the most recent changes in that context and what they portend for the future viability of geoengineering as a climate change abatement policy.

Geoengineering

Geoengineering, for purposes of this chapter, refers to climate engineering. Thus, while conceptually linked to a variety of weather modification schemes (such as cloud seeding to induce rain) dating back as far as the 1830's (Fleming, 2006), the proposals discussed here differ in that they aim to modify global climate rather than regional weather. Over the years a wide variety of number of such proposals have been advanced (for fuller discussion of particular approaches, see NOAA, 2012; Vaughan and Lenton, 2011; Fleming, 2010; Royal Society, 2009; Schneider, 2001; Keith, 2000). Broadly speaking, the major proposals involve either the management of solar radiation or the removal of carbon dioxide. Solar radiation management (SRM) projects counteract temperature rise by limiting the amount of sunlight that reaches the earth. Proposed ideas include mimicking the actions of volcanic ash through stratospheric sulphur aerosols; increasing the earth's albedo (amount of reflected light) by painting roofs and highways light colors or spraying water on the arctic ice cap in order to thicken the ice and reduce the rate at which it melts; enhancing the amount of cloud cover or its reflectivity through cloud seeding or using fine sea water spray to whiten the clouds; or building space-based mirrors or other structures designed to shade the earth. Carbon dioxide removal (CDR) technologies aim to reduce the level of greenhouse gasses in the atmosphere. Proposed ideas include various schemes for carbon capture and storage as well as proposals to fertilize the oceans with iron in order to stimulate a phytoplankton bloom and, hence, remove additional carbon dioxide from the atmosphere. Significantly, the major SRM approaches are far more powerful, faster, cheaper and pose greater risks than CDR technologies (Royal Society, 2009).

Figures 4b and 4c present data documenting the rapid and recent emergence of interest in geoengineering. Figure 4b displays Google Trends data capturing the volume of news references to 'geoengineering' in the publications that Google News tracks (lower graph) and the volume of internet searches for the term (upper graph). Taken together, these graphs show how recently the concept has entered public

91

awareness. News coverage of the concept was non-existent prior to 2006, minimal from 2006-2008, and showed a sharp increase in April 2009 when a high level Obama administration official (John Holdren, Director of the Office of Science and Technology Policy) indicated interest in the idea (Jha, 2009). Widespread public awareness of the concept, as indicated by increases in internet search volume, corresponded with the uptick in news coverage in April 2009.

Figure 4c tracks the level of scientific interest in the topic as measured by the number of publications about geoengineering present in the Web of Science database. The data show a long period of low level interest, from 1992 to 2005, followed by a rapid increase in attention to the concept starting in 2006. Comparison of the Figures 2 and 3 shows a) that there existed a long period of under-the-radar discussion of the concept within the scientific literature that was not noticed by the news media, b) that niche media outlets (e.g., science journalists) noted the uptick in scientific interest in geoengineering at the time that it happened (2006), and c) that it took several years of increased attention within the scientific community and the Obama administration's trial balloon that they were considering support of the idea before the concept reached the general public in 2009.

Figure 4b. Search and News reference volume for Geoengineering

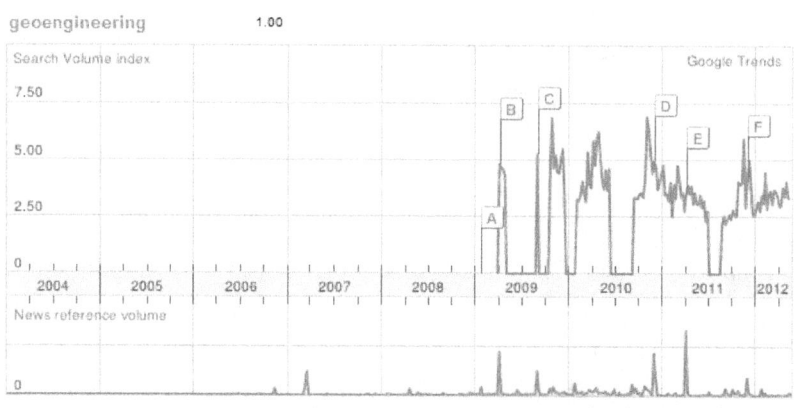

Source: Google Trends.

92

Figure 4c. Number of Scientific Publications Discussing Geoengineering, by Date of Publication: 1992-2012

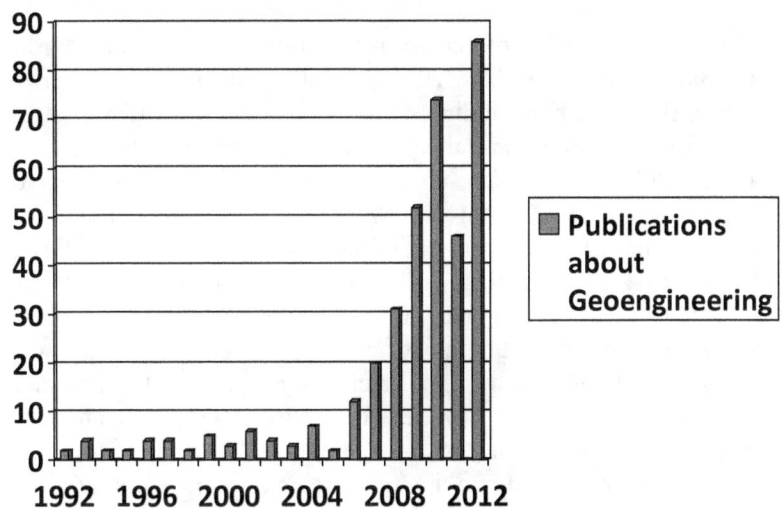

Data Source: Web of Science.

Indeed, the period of low level interest within the scientific community extends significantly further than the graph shows. The term 'geoengineering' was first used in the sense discussed here by Marchetti (1977). The date and context of this publication are noteworthy. Scientifically, the 1970's were a period characterized by an increased interest in the changing chemical composition of the atmosphere and sharp disagreements over the consequences of those changes. Some (Meadows, et. al., 1972) pointed to the possibility of anthropogenic warming from increased CO_2, while others argued that the increasing levels of aerosols in the atmosphere were producing global cooling (Gwynn, 1975). In other words, geoengineering solutions to global warming were being proposed well before there existed a scientific consensus on the existence of the problem. In this light, it is also worth noting that Marchetti's proposal was published in the first issue of a new journal, Climatic Change, whose editorial intention was to foster interdisciplinary communication about climate change.

Geoengineering's Problems

The quantitative data presented in the previous section clearly document a rapid and dramatic increase in the attention given to geoengineering proposals -- both as indicated by the extent of attention within the scientific community and the spread of discussion to the wider public -- around 2009. Those data, however, do little to explain either the long period of low-level discussion within the scientific community or the dramatic increase in recent attention. The central points of this sections are a) that geoengineering was seen from the outset as beset by a series of scientific, technical and ethical problems which marginalized the approach within the scientific community, b) that subsequent developments in science and technology have not eliminated those problems and, hence, c) new developments in the science and technology of geoengineering cannot be used to explain the shift of geoengineering out of the margins and into the mainstream of climate policy discussions.

While there have been modifications and refinements of the various geoengineering proposals through time, most of the basic ideas date from the late 60's-80's (Vaughan and Lenton, 2011; Fleming, 2010; Royal Society, 2009' Schneider, 2001; Keith, 2000). However, with few exceptions (such as the 1997 Wall Street Journal op-ed 'Why not do that?' by physicist Edward Teller, the father of the hydrogen bomb) the proposals were marginalized in the scientific community and ignored by the general public. There were three basic reasons for this. First, the ideas were perceived as speculative and as a distraction from attempts to gain international cooperation to slash emissions (Morton, 2007). Second, many of the techniques were not well understood and there were concerns about the uncertainties and/or potential side effects (Vaughan and Lenton, 2011; Fleming, 2010; Royal Society, 2009' Schneider, 2001; Keith, 2000). Thus, for example, the notion of pumping sulphur into the atmosphere to mimic the effects of a volcano has been criticized on the grounds that much of the sulphur will precipitate into the ocean and change the ocean's chemical balance. Third, a number of prominent scientists had moral or philosophical reservations. As Hans Fichter, a climate modeller at the Max Planck Institute for Meteorology, noted "the role of a geoscientist is to understand nature, not to change it" (Morton, 2007). In sum, while the specific objections raised varied from one proposal to another, none of the proposals have been demonstrated to work at the scale necessary to affect the climate and all were seen as suffering from a variety of scientific, technical, legal, moral, social and ethical objections (Schneider, 2008).

In the mid 2000's, however, a series of changes occurred. The idea of geoengineering began to gain traction in the scientific community following its endorsement by two Nobel laureates, Paul Crutzen and Ralph Cicerone (Morton, 2007). Broad (2006) provides a concise description of the change:

> [Prior to 2006] "their proposals were relegated to the fringes of climate science. Few journals would publish them. Few government agencies would pay for feasibility studies. Environmentalists and mainstream scientists said the focus should be on reducing greenhouse gases and preventing global warming in the first place. But now, in a major reversal, some of the world's most prominent scientists say the proposals deserve a serious look because of growing concerns about global warming. Worried about a potential planetary crisis, these leaders are calling on governments and scientific groups to study exotic ways to reduce global warming, seeing them as possible fallback positions if the planet eventually needs a dose of emergency cooling."

In contrast to the earlier phases, where discussion of geoengineering both rose and fell within the confines of the scientific community, the recent discussion has migrated from the scientific to other domains. This migration has involved a series of stages. In stage one, as noted above, several high-profile scientists embraced the idea, leading to coverage of the idea in the news sections of prominent scientific journals like Nature (Morton, 2007) and major newspapers like the New York Times (Broad, 2006). In the second stage, the idea was embraced by a number of public intellectuals. Thus, for example, Homer-Dixon and Keith (2008) argued against the all or nothing approach (either we do it full scale or we don't do it at all) and advocated limited small-scale testing to find out what works best in the event that such approaches must be used, an approach similarly endorsed by the Royal Society (2009). The need for practical knowledge about the techniques also follows from Dyer's (2008) suggestion that small-island nations or other countries facing existential threats might unilaterally implement such measures. In the third and most current phase, the idea has become a mainstay of policy debate and, as evidenced by a spate of recent books aimed at the literate public (Hamilton, 2014; Keith, 2013; Goodell, 2010; Brand, 2010; Fleming, 2010; Kintisch, 2010; Parkinson, 2010; Pielke, 2010), a topic of public interest.

To summarize, geoengineering experienced a mini-wave in the 1980's. The wave quickly crested as geoengineering was marginalized within the scientific community because of issues, among others, of cost, feasibility, uncertainty and risk, as well as philosophical objections to the attempt to play 'God.' Despite the fact that little has changed to ameliorate these concerns (Rickels, 2011; Parkinson, 2010; Kintisch, 2010; Goodell, 2010), a substantial portion of the scientific community has recently embraced the idea of geoengineering and introduced it into both public and policy discourse. What accounts for this second wave of interest? If changes in the science and technology haven't done away with the concerns that previously marginalized geoengineering within the scientific community, then other factors must be responsible. Thus, it is to the changing context of climate science and international climate policy that we now turn.

Climate Science

As previously noted, while there was considerable debate during the 1970's over whether the earth was warming or cooling, few people on either side of the debate saw anthropogenic factors as the major driver. Concern about the possibility of anthropogenic climate change became a major topic of scientific investigation in the late 1980's. The general trajectory of scientific understanding of the phenomena from that point to the present can be characterized as involving the reduction of scientific uncertainty about a) whether or not the climate was changing and b) whether or not humans were responsible for the change and, as a result, the emergence of a broad consensus within the international scientific community about the reality of anthropogenically caused climate change. Three distinct lines of evidence support this characterization.

First, this trajectory is evident in the selected quotes from the series of Intergovernmental Panel on Climate Change reports summarizing the current state of climate change science (Table 4a).

Table 4a. Increasing Certainty about the Existence of Anthropogenic Climate Change as Captured in Selected Quotes from the Five IPCC Reports

IPCC Report	Key Conclusions / Quotations
1st Assessment (1990-92)	There is a natural greenhouse effect, humans are contributing to more greenhouse gasses, the implications of this are unclear.
2nd Assessment (1995)	Climate has changed over the past century and is expected to continue changing. "The balance of evidence suggests a discernible human influence on global climate."
3rd Assessment (2001)	"An increasing body of observations gives a collective picture of a warming world and other changes in the climate system." " There is new and stronger evidence that most of the warming observed over the last 50 years is attributable to human activities."
4th	"Warming of the climate system is unequivocal."

Assessment (2007)	"Most of the observed increase in global average temperatures since the mid-20th century is *very likely* due to the observed increase in anthropogenic greenhouse gas concentrations."
5th Assessment (2013)	" Warming of the climate system is unequivocal." " Human influence on the climate system is clear... Human influence has been detected in warming of the atmosphere and the ocean, in changes in the global water cycle, in reductions in snow and ice, in global mean sea level rise, and in changes in some climate extremes. This evidence for human influence has grown since AR4. It is *extremely likely* that human influence has been the dominant cause of the observed warming since the mid-20th century."

These quotes indicate an increased certainty about both the empirical phenomena (the climate is warming) and the cause (various human activities). Second, during the 80s and 90s, when the level of scientific uncertainty was higher, scientific associations did not take official positions. However, in the past few years a number of scientific associations issued statements concluding that the evidence for human modification of climate is compelling (American Meteorological Society, 2003; American Geophysical Union, 2003; American Association for the Advancement of Science). Third, Oreskes (2004) examined 928 papers about climate change published in refereed scientific journals between 1993 and 2003. "The 928 papers were divided into six categories: explicit endorsement of the consensus position, evaluation of impacts, mitigation proposals, methods, paleoclimate analysis, and rejection of the consensus position. Of all the papers, 75% fell into the first three categories, either explicitly or implicitly accepting the consensus view; 25% dealt with methods or paleoclimate, taking no position on current anthropogenic climate change. Remarkably, none of the papers disagreed with the consensus position."

As scientific knowledge has increased, uncertainties have remained, but they are tied to increasingly more specific questions. Thus, in the early years of the global warming debate (1980's - early 1990's) attention focused on the broadest question: Is the global climate changing? By the mid-1990's, that question had largely been answered in the affirmative, but there were still significant doubts about the cause and, hence, the focal uncertainty was whether or not human activities were responsible. At the present time, the existence of and anthropogenic origin of climate change are not seriously questioned within the scientific community. The bulk of current scientific debate surrounds a much narrower question: How extensive will the change be and how rapid will it occur? In particular, the past 10-15 years have seen a substantial focus on the possibility of 'tipping points', i.e. possible positive feedback loops that could lead to comparatively quick changes in climate; e.g., rising Arctic temperatures leading to thaws that release methane into the atmosphere, thus increasing the greenhouse effect and starting the cycle over again (National Science Foundation, 2010).

In sum, the general trajectory of climate science over the past 25 years has underscored both the reality and the immediacy of the problem. On the one hand, scientists have become increasingly certain about the reality of anthropogenically generated climate change. On the other hand, as understanding of climate science deepened, the possibility of more immediate and dramatic changes resulting from rapid, non-linear changes in the climate became more widely accepted. Thus, shifts in scientific knowledge implied both a) the need to do something to address the problem and b) the possibility that change would come so rapidly that adaptation would not be as viable as response as previously believed. Changes in scientific knowledge alone, however, do little to explain the shift away from mitigation approaches and toward geoengineering. For this, we turn to an examination of international climate policy.

International Climate Policy

Climate change, as a global problem, can only be mitigated through a global response. No individual country, no matter how large a carbon

99

emitter, can resolve the problem on their own. However, in the late 1980's, when climate change was initially identified as a potential problem, the institutional structure for a global response did not exist. This section briefly recounts the history of attempts to forge such a structure and argues that the consensus on how to proceed that characterized most of the period from the late-1980's on has recently fallen apart.

Broadly speaking, the structure for addressing global environmental problems can be traced to the World Commission on Environment and Development (WCED) which was commissioned by the UN in 1983 to discuss the environment and development as a single issue or, in other words, to facilitate a rapprochement between the global north (whose high levels of consumption were blamed for environmental degradation by the global south) and the global south (whose high levels of population growth were rendered as the primary problem by the north). The most significant legacy of the group's work was the publication of *Our Common Future* (1987) and the popularization of the term 'sustainable development.' In an attempt to reconcile the differences between the north and the south, the report made two major points. First, development was still desirable, but unlimited development for all was recognized as biophysically impossible and, hence, future development should be sustainable development. Second, the countries of the developed north have already received significant economic benefits from the exploitation of natural resources and, hence, they should take the first steps in addressing global environmental problems while the less developed countries of the global south would be given more leeway in the pursuit of economic development. Stated another way, there was both a recognition of the need for restrictions on growth and an ethical consensus on how to achieve those restrictions.

The development of an institutional structure specific to climate change can be traced to the UN Framework Convention on Climate Change (UNFCC) produced at the Rio Earth Summit of June, 1992. The objective of the convention was to stabilize greenhouse gas emissions at a level that would prevent human induced climate change. While the agreement lacked any strict limits or enforcement mechanism, it is notable for three major reasons: 1) it established internationally agreed upon methods for collecting and distributing data on greenhouse gas emissions (leading to the IPCC reports quoted in the previous section), 2) the treaty called for updates (known as Protocols) aimed at setting mandatory emissions limits and providing enforcement mechanisms and 3) it divided the signatory countries into three groups with differing responsibilities: 23 industrialized countries, 17 'countries in transition' and developing countries (the remainder of the signatories). This division reflects the ethical consensus reached by the WCED: the developed countries were required to accept limitations while developing countries were not, though developing countries could become subject to emissions limits when they were sufficiently developed.

The Kyoto Protocol, negotiated in December 1997, updated and extended the UNFCC. In it most industrialized nations and some central European economies in transition agreed to legally binding reductions in greenhouse gas emissions of an average of 6 to 8% below 1990 levels between the years 2008-2012, defined as the first emissions budget period. Three points merit specific attention. First, the Protocol followed the UNFCC structure: countries classified as industrialized or in transition agreed to binding reductions, while developing countries were not expected to make such commitments. Second, the Protocol, following the model of the 1987 Montreal Protocol on Substances that Deplete the Ozone Layer and the US experience with SOx/NOx reduction under the Clean Air Act, adopted variety of flexibility mechanisms that included a 'cap and trade' strategy for achieving the stated emission targets. Third, the specific reduction targets agreed to by the various countries were reached following Vice President Al Gore's arrival in Kyoto with a US proposal to reduce its total emissions an average of 7% below 1990 levels; a proposal that significantly went beyond what other countries expected the US to agree to and which broke a negotiating impasse that had existed to that time. However, neither the Clinton administration nor the Bush administration sent the protocol to Congress for ratification. The Bush administration explicitly rejected the protocol in 2001.

The 15th Conference of the UNFCC Parties (COP 15) took place in December 2009 in Copenhagen. This conference was expected to be the follow-up to Kyoto; where a treaty extending beyond the 2012 end date of Kyoto (i.e., the second emissions budget period) would be agreed upon. Instead, the conference ended in chaos as a result of the confrontation between the US and China -- the two largest contributors to global emissions, neither of which is bound by the provisions of the Kyoto Protocol. On December 17, Secretary of State Hillary Clinton outlined the details of a US proposal aimed at 'breaking the impasse' in the existing negotiations. That proposal had two key provisions: 1) support for an initiative to mobilize $100 billion per year by 2020 for developing countries to help them mitigate the impacts of climate change and 2) pressuring developing countries to agree to emissions cuts along with the industrialized world for the first time. The Chinese adamantly opposed the US proposal.

In short, the negotiations broke down over a dispute between the two largest emitters, China and the US (neither of which had ratified Kyoto), on the nature of the path forward. While not part of the formal Kyoto agreement, the general expectation was that a) the developed countries would fulfill their commitment and b) the next major agreement (i.e., the Copenhagen agreement) would broaden the number of countries accepting emissions limits to include some of the developing countries that were not covered by Kyoto. Viewed in the context of this history, the US proposal aimed to divide the developing world into two camps: a) China and other rapidly developing countries (who would be expected to commit to emissions cuts) and b) the rest of the developing world (which would receive a large amount of aid and not be expected to make emission cuts). The Chinese response was designed to maintain their status as a developing country not expected to make emissions reductions (Lynas, 2009).

In both cases, these countries are responding to internal political pressures. The Obama administration knew that it has no chance of getting an international agreement ratified by the Senate unless it covered China. The politics of this have been clear for over a decade. In 1997, by a vote of 95 to 0, the Senate passed the Byrd-Hagel Resolution which stated that the Senate would not ratify Kyoto if developing countries were not required to participate on the same timetable. Thus, the Obama administration was attempting to divide and conquer the developing countries in a strategic move aimed at getting an agreement that could be ratified by the US Senate. From the Chinese point of view, it is unreasonable to expect China and other developing nations to commit to emission reductions at this point when the US has not formally agreed to emissions reductions (i.e., to 'go first' as expected by the UNFCC process) and most of the developing country signatories have failed to meet their Kyoto commitments.

To summarize, the UN member nations reached broad consensus on an ethical framework for international agreements on the environment and development before climate change emerged as a major issue. When it did, the basic structure of that framework was incorporated into the UNFCC process. Similarly, following on the success of the Montreal Protocol (which limited ozone depleting substances) and the US experience lowering SOx/NOx under the provisions of the Clean Air Act, there was general agreement on the appropriate policy vehicle for dealing with climate change, a variety of 'flexibility mechanisms' which included, as one element of the package, a cap-and-trade system. These two pieces became the central components of the Kyoto Protocol. Stated another way, the early years of the international climate change discussions were characterized by consensus on both the ethical structure and the policy instrument. A crack in this consensus appeared when the US failed to ratify Kyoto, though the ongoing support of the Democratic party for Kyoto led the rest of the world to hope that the US would ultimately join and, hence, acted to minimize the significance attributed to the crack. By the mid-2000's, as the emissions of China and India continued to increase, the Democrats realized that it was politically impossible to get the US to ratify an agreement structured like Kyoto. This led not only to the Obama administration position at Copenhagen, but also to the embrace of a carbon tax (rather than a cap-and-trade system) by such notables as Nobel economist Joseph Steiglitz, the former head of Clinton's Council of Economic Advisors (Stiglitz, 2006). In other words, a complete break from the earlier consensus.

From Mitigation to Geoengineering

Framed in relation to the concepts in Figure 1, there has been a recent and relatively abrupt shift in international climate change policy discussions. Prior to 2009 discussions focused almost entirely on mitigation, with some planning for adaptation and an almost total absence of serious consideration of geoengineering. Since 2009, climate policy discussions have placed much more equal emphasis on all three intervention strategies (mitigation, adaptation, geoengineering). While it would be an overstatement to suggest that geoengineering has attained a policy emphasis rivaling mitigation, there can be little doubt that there has been a dramatic increase in willingness to consider it as a strategy worth pursuing. This change in the level of interest in geoengineering approaches is represented diagrammatically by the green line in Figure 4d.

Figure 4d. Historical Changes in Three Areas of Climate Change Discourse

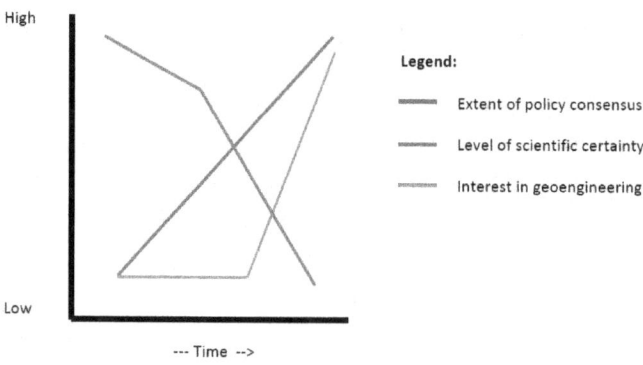

What accounts for this shift? Among the public the conventional answer is that these are new ideas, that scientists have just recently come up with these proposals. They could not have been considered previously because they did not exist prior to their entry into the policy debate. However, as we have seen, this is not the case. Geoengineering proposals can be traced back to as early as 1977. Despite knowledge of them, they remained marginalized from serious policy consideration by a myriad scientific, technical, social, economic, legal and ethical concerns. Viewed this way, the question can be posed in a slightly different manner: why are geoengineering proposals no longer marginalized? At first blush, one might suspect that enhanced scientific understanding, better technology, and other similar factors have developed over time and, hence, the earlier concerns about geoengineering are no longer valid. This, again, turns out not to be the case. The same controversies that plagued geoengineering proposals from the outset continue to plague them today. Thus, if changes in science and technology can't account for the move of geoengineering ideas from the margin to the center of policy debate, we must look elsewhere. As represented in Figure 4, the increased interest in geoengineering must be understood in relation to other contextual changes.

Significantly, the emergence of interest in geoengineering wasn't the only change in climate policy discussions occurring in the mid-2000s. For the bulk of the period prior to 2006, the vast majority of the mitigation discussion focused on a relatively narrow band of policy options defined by the Framework Convention on Climate Change: flexibility mechanisms involving a global roll out through time in which the developed countries were expected to make the initial reductions in emissions leading to subsequent commitments to emissions reductions by the less developed countries. Circa 2006 certain progressive economists (Steiglitz, 2006) began advocating for an alternative mitigation strategy, a carbon tax, which was subsequently embraced in a number of areas (e.g., British Columbia in 2008, Australia in 2011). The shift away from cap-and-trade approaches and toward a carbon tax can be seen, like the emerging interest in geoengineering, as a reflection of decreased confidence in the traditional consensus approach.

What is hard to appreciate from the perspective of recent history, given the total lack of political progress on addressing climate change over the past 15 years, is the rapidity with which the international community moved toward collective action early in the process. Scientists began researching the question in earnest in the early 1980s, but their findings at that time did more to elucidate the complex interplay of factors relevant to understanding the problem than to providing any definitive clarification of the actual situation. Public awareness of the issue during the early 1980s was virtually non-existent. Only after the heat wave of the summer of 1988 did a majority (58%) of the American public report ever having heard of the 'greenhouse effect' (Nisbett and Myers, 2007). However, only a decade later, the world's leaders stood together and congratulated themselves as they signed the Kyoto Protocol in 1997. In slightly more than a decade, climate change went from a non-issue to being understood as a issue of such significance that an innovative international policy regime which appeared capable of addressing the issue had been negotiated. This dramatic progress was possible only because the existing building blocks for such an accord were already in place by 1987: the successful US experience with SOx/NOx reduction, the international agreement that successfully limited ozone destroying aerosols and the Brundtland Commission report, the result of over a decade of international negotiation, that outlined an ethical consensus on how global environmental problems should be addressed. As such, the Kyoto Protocol was widely viewed as the natural extension of a process that had previously yielded demonstrable success.

Viewed retrospectively, it is easy to see that the optimism which greeted Kyoto was misplaced. Constructing an effective policy regime aimed at a central pillar of the modern economy (fossil fuels) turned out to be much harder than implementing one targeted at SOx/NOx or the small number of ozone depleting chemicals for which the manufacturers rapidly developed alternatives and, as a result, profited from the switch and supported the regime (i.e., the Montreal Protocol). Similarly, there was evidence early on that the ethical consensus negotiated in Brundtland was not always consistent with national politics and, as a result, it took until 2005 for the Protocol to be ratified and become official (significantly, without the participation of the US which was, at the time, the world's largest emitter of carbon). This period of slowly degrading policy consensus is captured in Figure 4 by the portion of the blue line that is slowly descending. Whatever optimism remained about the viability of the Kyoto process dissipated rapidly once it became clear that the policy had not been particularly effective (many of the signatory countries were failing to meet their emissions targets) and that the likelihood of extending the process into the next timeframe (as was supposed to happen at the 2010 Copenhagen meeting) was slight. This period of rapid descent into policy divergence is represented by the sharply falling portion of the blue line in Figure 4.

While the declining policy consensus, particularly as it relates to the mitigation strategy proposed in the Kyoto process, is a necessary factor for understanding the rise in interest in geoengineering, it is not sufficient. Specifically, the decline in enthusiasm for the Kyoto process took place gradually over a number of years and, hence, provides little insight for the meteoric rise in interest in geoengineering. Thus, it is important to also contextualize geoengineering's rise in relation to the changes in climate science. As depicted by the rising red line in Figure 4, there has been a consistent increase in the scientific certainty about the reality of climate change and the role of humans as the cause. Equally as significant, recent research has drawn attention to the possibility that the climate may change in a rapid, dramatic and non-linear manner rather than slow and incrementally. If so, then adaptation becomes a much less viable strategy.

Taking developments in both climate science and international climate policy into consideration provides the basis for understanding the rapid rise in interest in geoengineering. Early on there was both uncertainty about the nature of the climate problem and faith in the ability of the political process to successfully negotiate an effective international mitigation strategy. In this context, mitigation seemed a viable strategy and there was no reason to embrace geoengineering and its myriad scientific, technical, social, legal, and ethical concerns. As time progressed, concern about the severity of climate change increased while faith in the ability of the international community to devise a viable political solution to mitigate the problem declined. At a certain point, these trends intersected creating a tipping point that resulted in the dramatic uptick in interest in geoengineering, i.e., in a technological solution that seemed not to require international political negotiations. In other words, while the problems which had earlier marginalized geoengineering proposals were still understood as being as significant as ever, in the new context these problems were seen by many as more manageable and, in particular, more controllable than as the vicissitudes of negotiating an effective policy designed to mitigate the climate problem. This "it's a bad option, but it's better than the alternatives" take on the situation is explicitly present in the editorial by Nobel laureate Paul Cruitzen (2006), the article which many point to as a turning point in public consideration of geoengineering:

> By far the preferred way to resolve the policy makers' dilemma is to lower the emissions of the greenhouse gases. However, so far, attempts in that direction have been grossly unsuccessful. ... Therefore, although by far not the best solution, the usefulness of artificially enhancing earth's albedo and thereby cooling climate by adding sunlight reflecting aerosol in the stratosphere (Budyko, 1977; NAS, 1992) might again be explored and debated as a way to ... counteract the climate forcing of growing CO_2 emissions.

As the quote makes clear, Cruitzen's injection of geoengineering into policy debates was an explicit reaction to the failure of mitigation policy. The ubiquity of this reasoning has been widely recognized (Hamilton, 2014; Keith, 2013; Brand, 2010; Goodell, 2010; Kintisch, 2010; Pielke, 2010). When the science of climate change was uncertain and a political agreement on mitigation seemed feasible, the scientific and engineering community kept the geoengineering option in the margins. However, as the scientific community became more certain about the science and the need for action and came to see the politicians as unwilling or unable to devise a viable mitigation strategy, a number of leading scientists

108

decided to interject themselves into the policy debate in a way that, to them, made sense; by shifting the discourse on how to address climate change from mitigation focus controlled by the politicians to a geoengineering focus where scientists and engineers exert more power and control over what happens. Interestingly, this set of contextual factors has created an odd coalition of geoengineering advocates ranging from well known environmentalists (Brand, 2010) through middle-of - the-road scientific bodies (Royal Society, 2009) to individuals representing conservative think tanks (Thernstrum, 2010) and even climate deniers who perceived an opportunity to make money (Hamilton, 2014).

Stated another way, the widespread recognition of the ethical rupture which underlay the collapse of the Kyoto process led to a growing sense of disillusionment with the idea that the nations of the world would be able to generate the social ingenuity necessary to effectively address the problem via mitigation. It was in this context that geoengineering, an approach which seems to place relatively greater emphasis on scientific and technical ingenuity and relatively less emphasis on social ingenuity, rose to prominence as a viable option. However, within the relatively few years that geoengineering has been subjected to intense scrutiny, it has become increasingly clear that this is not the case. Given the widespread recognition of the potential for large-scale unintended consequences, policy deliberations have focused on devising strategies for small scale testing while avoiding rogue deployment of geoengineering technologies. It is for this reason that the World Economic Forum 's (2013: 57) assessment of global risks identifies "rogue deployment of geoengineering technology" rather than geoengineering technology as the source of global risk. Specifically, discussions have focused upon two broad areas in which geoengineering technologies will require social innovation. First, as Curvelo (2013) has noted, "the self-assertive invasion of nature's various domains, the scale and complexity of the technoscientific tasks involved, the unpredictable long-term impacts of geoengineering actions, and the huge uncertainties that these proposals raise point to a shift in the nature of human action that requires a commensurate ethics of foresight and responsibility." She

109

argues that geoengineering proposals imply two kinds of "epochal break". From the earth science perspective, they imply a further break in the human-earth relationship; a shift from the unanticipated intrusion of humans into earth systems process associated with the Anthropocene to an era involving intentional manipulation of the system. Similarly, such proposals also represent a fundamental break in the relationship among science, technology and society. In light of these considerations and the fundamental issues they raise for democratic process, a dialog has arisen around the need for public engagement prior to deployment (see, for example, Parkhill and Pidgeon, 2011; NERC, 2010).

Secondly, as the following example illustrates, the governance issue has turned out to be much more complicated than initially believed. In 2007, the Planktos Corporation announced it was going to conduct an iron fertilization experiment off the coast of the Gallapagos Islands. Several groups submitted briefs to the Scientific Group of the London Convention and Protocol which, under the United Nations Convention on the Law of the Sea, regulates ocean dumping and other forms of marine pollution. These objections ultimately stopped the Planktos experiment and led to the creation in 2010 of a regulatory framework covering iron fertilization, a framework that is currently being elaborated to include other forms of marine geoengineering (Bodle, 2013). Similarly, in 2010 the Convention on Biological Diversity adopted provisions calling for member parties to abstain from geoengineering unless the parties have fully considered the risks and impacts of those activities on biodiversity (UNEP-CBD, 2012). Hearings by both the British (House of Commons, 2010; Secretary of State for Energy and Climate Change, 2010) and American governments (US House of Representatives, 2010; USGAO, 2010a, 2010b) have highlighted the need for a framework governing the deployment of geoengineering technologies. Similar concerns led a global network of NGOs to establish The Solar Radiation Management Governance Initiative aimed at developing a governance framework for all SRM technologies. Debate within the group has been lively, with the recognition that the process will become even more so as additional groups are drawn into the discussion (SRMGI, 2011). Thus, in a very short time, the need for substantial public and government involvement

110

in the governance and regulation of geoengineering technology has become evident. All these factors have led the IPCC (2014: Chapter 6, 91) to tentatively conclude: "The potential role of geoengineering as a viable component of climate policy is yet to be determined."

To summarize, there have been two waves of technological optimism involving geoengineering. The first occurred in the late 70s and early 80s. However, that wave quickly receded as the scientific, political, social, ethical and economic problems associated with the various technological proposals became evident. Despite the fact that those issues were not resolved, a second wave of interest in these proposals began in 2006 and extends to the present. Two contextual factors were responsible: 1) the increasing consensus that climate change represents a major problem with the potential to occur more rapidly and with greater consequence than previously believed and 2) the collapse of the Copenhagen summit and associated recognition that the ethical consensus which underpinned the UNFCC process had dissolved and, hence, progress on international mitigation policy would not go forward in the near term. In this light, geoengineering proposals attracted attention because they seemed to provide a way forward that minimized engagement with the broken political process associated with mitigation policy.

The past few years, however, have shown this optimism to be misplaced. It may, in fact, be harder to get political agreement on geoenginering proposals than on mitigation. The science of emission reductions is well understood, the technologies already exist, the negative impacts of those technologies are small relative to the consequences of fossil fuels, and the changes needed to reduce emissions have a large number of co-benefits: energy security, national security, a healthier environment, economic competitiveness and job creation. In contrast, the science surrounding most geoengineering proposals is not well known, few of the technologies have actually been developed, liability for harmful effects could be a legal nightmare, and no international institutions or arrangements exist to authorize small-scale field tests, much less large-scale deployment. Presuming that the same social dynamics that governed the first wave continue to operate, as these facts become more widely understood by the general public, the current wave of enthusiasm for geoenginnering will also recede. Given the recognition of the need to act on climate change, it is unlikely that interest in geoengineering technologies will disappear. It is, however, probable that these technologies (especially SRM technologies) will remain a "Plan B," a fall back option to be used only if mitigation and adaptation are insufficient, rather than becoming primary policy option. There is no way the epochal breaks associated with geoengineering technologies (Curvelo, 2013) can be achieved without significant social ingenuity. Any remaining optimism that there exists a simple technological fix for the climate problem is profoundly misplaced.

References

Bodle, Ralph. 2013. "Climate Law and Geoengineering." Pages 447-470 in Hollo, Erkki J., Kulovesi, Kati, and Mehling, Michael (Eds.) *Climate Change and the Law*. Springer.

Bracmort, Kelsi and Lattanzio, Richard. 2013. Geoengineering: Governance and Technology Policy. Congressional Research Service R41371.

Brand, Stuart. 2010. *Whole Earth Discipline: Why Dense Cities, Nuclear Power, Transgenic Crops, Restored Wildlands, and Geoengineering Are Necessary*. Penguin Books.

Broad, William. 2006. "How to cool a planet (maybe)." *New York Times*. June 27. http://www.nytimes.com/2006/06/27/science/earth/27cool.html?_r=1&ex=1151985600&en=ca9e39a26d7e4ece&ei=5065&partner=MYWAY

Crutzen Paul J. 2006. "Albedo enhancement by stratospheric sulphur injections: a contribution to resolve a policy dilemma? An Editorial Essay." *Climatic Change* 77(3–4): 211–219

Dyer, Gwynne. 2008. *Climate Wars*. Random House Canada.

Fleming , James Rodger . 2010. *Fixing the Sky: The Checkered History of Weather and Climate Control*. New York: Columbia University Press.

Goodell, Jeff. 2010. *How to Cool the Planet: Geoengineering and the Audacious Quest to Fix Earth's Climate*. NY: Houghton Mifflin Harcourt.

Gwynn, Peter. 1975. "The Cooling World." Newsweek. April 28. Page

64.

Jha, Alok. 2009. "Obama climate adviser open to geo-engineering to tackle global warming." *The Guardian,* April 8. Retrieved from http://www.theguardian.com/environment/2009/apr/08/geo-engineering-john-holdren

Haluza-Delay, Randolph and Debra J. Davidson. 2008. "The environment and a globalizing sociology." *Canadian Journal of Sociology* 33(3): 631-656.

Hamilton, Clive. 2014. *Earthmasters: The Dawn of the Age of Climate Engineering.* New Haven: Yale University Press.

Homer-Dixon, Thomas and David Keith. 2008. "Blocking the sky to save the earth." *New York Times,* September 20. http://www.homerdixon.com/articles/20080920-nytimes-blockingthesky.html

House of Commons. Science and Technology Committee. 2009. *Engineering: Turning Ideas into Reality.* London: The Stationery Office Limited.

House of Commons. Science and Technology Committee. 2010. *The Regulation of Geoengineering.* London: The Stationery Office Limited.

International Panel on Climate Change (IPCC). 1992. *First Assessment Overview Report.* Retrieved from http://www.ipcc.ch/ipccreports/1992%20IPCC%20Supplement/IPCC_1990_and_1992_Assessments/English/ipcc_90_92_assessments_far_overview.pdf

----- 1995. *Second Assessment Report.* Climate Change 1995: Synthesis Report. Retrieved from http://www.ipcc.ch/pdf/climate-changes-1995/ipcc-2nd-assessment/2nd-assessment-en.pdf

----- 2001. Third Assessment Report. Climate Change 2001: Synthesis Report. Retrieved from http://www.ipcc.ch/ipccreports/tar/vol4/english/index.htm

----- 2007. *Fourth Assessment Report. Climate Change 2007: Synthesis Report.* Retrieved from http://www.ipcc.ch/report/ar4/

------ 2013. *Fifth Assessment Report. Climate Change 2013: The Physical Science Basis.* Retrieved from http://www.ipcc.ch/report/ar5/wg1/

------ 2014. *AR5 - WGIII Final Draft Report - Climate Change 2014: Mitigation of Climate Change.* Retrieved from http://www.ipcc.ch/report/ar5/wg3/

Keith, David. 2013. *A Case for Climate Engineering.* Cambridge: MIT Press.

------ 2000. "Geoengineering the climate: history and prospect." *Annual Review of Energy and Environment* 25:245–284

Kintisch, Eli. 2010. *Hack The Planet: Science's Best Hope - or Worst Nightmare - for Averting Climate Catastrophe.* Wiley.

Lynas, Mark. 2009. "How do I know China wrecked the Copenhagen deal? I was in the room." *The Guardian*, December 19. http://www.guardian.co.uk/environment/2009/dec/22/copenhagen-climate-change-mark-lynas

Meadows, D., et al., *"The Limits to Growth."* New York 1972.

Morton, Oliver. 2007. "Is this what it takes to save the world?" *Nature* 447(May 10): 132-136.

National Academy of Science. 1992. *Policy Implications of Greenhouse Warming: Mitigation, Adaptation, and the Science Base* , Committee on Science, Engineering, and Public Policy (COSEPUP)

Natural Environment Research Council (NERC) 2010. *Experiment Earth? Report on a Public Dialogue on Geoengineering.* Retrieved from http://www.nerc.ac.uk/about/consult/geoengineering.asp

National Science Foundation. 2010. "Methane releases from Arctic Shelf may be much larger and faster than anticipated." http://www.nsf.gov/news/news_summ.jsp?cntn_id=116532&org=NSF&from=news

Nisbett, Matthew and Teresa Myers. 2007. "Twenty Years of Public Opinion about Global Warming." *Public Opinion Quarterly*, Vol. 71, No. 3, Fall 2007, pp. 444–470.

National Oceanic and Atmospheric Administration (NOAA). 2012. *State of the Science Fact Sheet: Climate Engineering.* Ed.: U.S. Department of Commerce.

Oreskes, Naomi. 2004. "Beyond the Ivory Tower: The Scientific

Consensus on Climate Change." *Science* 3 December 2004: Vol. 306. no. 5702, p. 1686 DOI: 10.1126/science.1103618 http://www.sciencemag.org/cgi/content/full/306/5702/1686

Parkhill, Karen & Pidgeon, Nick. 2011. *Public Engagement on Geoengineering Research: Preliminary Report on the SPICE Deliberative Workshops* . Understanding Risk Working Paper 11-01. Retrieved from http://psych.cf.ac.uk/understandingrisk/docs/spice.pdf

Parkinson, Claire. 2010. *Coming Climate Crisis: Consider the Past, Beware the Big Fix.* Rowman & Littlefield.

Pielke Jr., Roger. 2010. *The Climate Fix: What Scientists and Politicians Won't Tell You About Global Warming.* New York: Basic Books.

Rickels, W.; Klepper, G.; Dovern, J.; Betz, G.; Brachatzek, N.; Cacean, S.; Güssow, K.; Heintzenberg J.; Hiller, S.; Hoose, C.; Leisner, T.; Oschlies, A.; Platt, U.; Proelß, A.; Renn, O.; Schäfer, S.; Zürn M. 2011. *Large-Scale Intentional Interventions into the Climate System? Assessing the Climate Engineering Debate.* Scoping report conducted on behalf of the German Federal Ministry of Education and Research (BMBF), Kiel Earth Institute, Kiel.

Royal Society. 2009. *Geoengineering the Climate: Science, Governance and Uncertainty.* London: The Royal Society.

Schneider, S.H. 2001. "Earth systems engineering and management." *Nature* 409(6818):417–421

Secretary of State for Energy and Climate Change. 2010. *Government Response to the House of Commons Science and Technology Committee 5th Report of Session 2009-10: The Regulation of Geoengineering.* London: The Stationery Office Limited

Schneider S.H. 2008. "Geoengineering: could we or should we make it work?" *Philosophical Transactions of the Royal Society A: Mathematical, Physical and Engineering Sciences* 366 3843–3862

Solar Radiation Management Governance Iniative (SRMGI). 2011. *Solar Radiation Management: The Governance of Research.* Retrieved from http://www.srmgi.org/files/2012/01/DES2391_SRMGI-report_web_11112.pdf

Stiglitz, Joseph. 2006. "A New Agenda for Global Warming," *The Economists' Voice*: Vol. 3 : Iss. 7, Article 3. DOI: 10.2202/1553-3832.1210

Thernstrom, Samuel. 2010. "Engineering Our Attitudes: How Geoengineering Can Inform Our Perspective on Climate Policy." Testimony before the American Academy for the Advancement of Science. Retrieved from: http://www.aei.org/article/energy-and-the-environment/climate-change/engineering-our-attitudes/

United Nations. 1987. *Report of the World Commission on Environment and Development: Our Common Future.* Retrieved from http://www.un-documents.net/wced-ocf.htm

---- 1992. *United Nations Framework Convention on Climate Change.* Retrieved from http://unfccc.int/resource/docs/convkp/conveng.pdf

UNEP-CBD. 2012. "Regulatory Framework for Climate-Related Geoengineering Relevant to the Convention on Biological Diversity." Retrieved from http://www.srmgi.org/files/2010/10/CBD-sbstta-report-16-inf-29-regulatory-legal-framework-for-geonengineering-2012.pdf

United States Government General Accounting Office (USGAO). 2010a. *Climate Change - Preliminary Observations on Geoengineering Science, Federal Efforts, and Governance Issues.* Testimony Before the Committee on Science and Technology, House of Representatives. F. W. Rusco. Washington, DC: United States Government Accountability Office.

---- 2010b. *Climate Change - A Coordinated Strategy Could Focus Federal Geoengineering Research and Inform Governance Efforts.* Report to the Chairman, Committee on Science and Technology, House of Representatives. Washington, DC: United States Government Accountability Office.

United States House of Representatives - Science and Technology Committee. 2010. *Engineering the Climate: Research Needs and Strategies for International Collaboration.* One Hundred

116

Eleventh Congress, Second session, October 2010. Washington, DC, United States House of Representatives.

Vaughan, Naomi and Timothy Lenton. 2011. "A review of climate geoengineering proposals." *Climatic Change* 109:745–790

Watts, Robert. 1997. *Engineering Response to Global Climate Change: Planning a Research and Development Agenda.* CRC Press.

World Economic Forum. 2013. *Global Risks 2013, Eighth Edition (An Initiative of the Risk Response Network)* Retrieved from http://www.weforum.org/reports/global-risks-2013-eighth-edition.

The Ecological and Social Implications of Invasive Alien Ideologies and Technologies: A Case Study of Oil and Gas Development in the Canadian Arctic

David McRobert(1)

Introduction

This chapter explores how Western-based ideas and ideologies about resource management, economic, legal, and socio-cultural systems have disrupted and destabilized non-Western Aboriginal societies (both Inuit and First Nations) in the Canadian Arctic and the sub-Arctic northern regions. For hundreds of years Western-based resource management concepts, technologies, values and ideas have been imposed on other societies, primarily through militaristic control of space and resource development as well as religious and educational systems. Western ideologies and values can be characterized as analogous to invasive alien (or exotic) species that are disruptive to existing ecosystems. The introduction of Western approaches to development has led to severe cultural and social destabilization in many traditional societies such as the hunter-gatherer Aboriginal populations in Canada. This destabilization has resulted in the loss of traditional social and economic frameworks. The loss of these frameworks undermines the ability of non-Western societies to maintain sustainable livelihoods and protect ecosystems that support them.

Specifically, this chapter considers the impact of alien ideals, laws, resource management systems and socio-technical systems related to the oil and gas development sector in the Canadian Arctic in the past, present, and future. It is argued that metropolitan interests in Southern Canada, to paraphrase Harold Innis (1930, 1972), exported a resource development paradigm to the Arctic that caused cultural, economic, political and social disruptions to Aboriginal peoples. To understand the development processes underway today and the social, cultural, political,

118

economic, and ecological destabilization of the Canadian North, it is necessary to consider some of the key social, cultural and economic transformations that have taken place in the past. The chapter then examines the current impact of alien ideologies and socio-technical systems on Aboriginal communities in the Arctic and on the natural environment. Finally, the chapter considers some of the future threats posed, such as the possible increase in Arctic shipping.

Invasive Alien Species

Invasive alien species encroach upon the territory of other species. Those alien species that thrive in their new habitat cause native species to relocate, weaken or die. Successful invasive species, like the zebra mussel, sea lamprey, and round goby are generally aggressive, extremely adaptable, and have high reproduction rates that enable them to spread quickly. Unchecked they can outcompete native species and cause imbalances in ecological systems and economic and social effects (Bates 1956; Mooney 2000).

According to experts invasive species have been invading the niches of other species for millions of years (Mooney 2000). The spread of alien invasive species has skyrocketed in the past 400 years and has been tightly connected with the evolution and expansion of global trade routes. Similarly, Western ideas, religions and educational frameworks, which can be characterized as invasive in their impact, have been aggressively shaping non-Western cultures for centuries.

Understanding Ecological History and Invasive Ideologies: Colinvaux's Insights

For most of their evolutionary development, humans lived as hunter-gatherers in relatively small groups. The majority of these societies evolved social, political and economic structures that favoured ecological patterns adapted to or in relative balance with natural systems. Due to a dependency on certain foods in a region and familiarity with spatial dimensions of specific locations, traditional communities were often unified and had tightly interconnected social relationships (Wilson 2012).

Traditional hunter-gatherers developed the tools and abilities to achieve modest livelihoods (Wilson 2012) and usually maintained a reasonable balance with local ecosystems.

The rapid spread of grain-based agriculture and its complex and alien technologies to remote locations inhabited by indigenous peoples in the past 500 years has had a staggering impact on the environment and the social fabric of their communities. (Harari 2014) Grain-based societies had developed particular ideas about property and social control that obfuscated the difference between wants and needs, and means and ends. Control of resources and land through colonization became a dominant pre-occupation as various European empires spread across the planet between the 15th and 20th centuries (Colinvaux 1980; Innis 1972). As grain-based societies moved away from more sustainable traditional livelihoods, and as Western ideologies and technologies spread, increasing pressure has been placed on the earth's carrying capacity (Colinvaux 1980; Harari 2014; Wilson 2012).

Colonizing societies are characterized by nichelessness (Portmann 1961) to the extent they are not firmly located in variable spatial and ecological niches and attempt to modify invaded landscapes rather than adapt to them and use the technologies (e.g. dog sleds and caribou insulated clothing and boots in the Arctic) developed by traditional societies such as the Inuit and Inuvialiut. Consequently they normally spread new ideas and ideologies about resource management, space, nature, religion, culture and human power relations, including gender balance, that serve to destabilize traditional societies. Unique cultural and ecological values are undermined, and traditional communities become vulnerable to social pressures associated with Western cultural norms and values. (2) Western ideologies, technologies and trade systems have not only destabilized traditional diets, social norms, and ideological frameworks, but also have physically introduced fatal and chronic viral diseases such as tuberculosis and nuisance species from Europe (e.g., rats and pigeons).

Socio-Ecological Transformations in the Canadian North

A. Marginalization and the Traditional Economy

One of the biggest impacts of Euro-Canadian colonization has been on the social, cultural and economic systems of Aboriginal societies (Zaslow 1971; Dacks 1981; Page 1986). As staple industries (e.g., fur trading, whaling, mining and petroleum extraction) developed in the North, these industries introduced varying degrees of social and economic disruption and dependency in the hinterland (Dacks 1981; Riddington 1982).

Anthropologist Hugh Brody (1975, 1983) has observed that the relationship between the metropolis and the Northern hinterland was determined "according to the wishes and ambitions of white outsiders, rather than by the gradual and selective process connoted by the term acculturation. Immense obstacles [have been] ... placed in the way of...[those who] preferred to retain their own...practices" (Brody 1975, 8).

B. Modernization and Oil and Gas Development in the North

At the regional level, mineral and petroleum development tends to generate a phenomenon that can be described as economic dualism where two distinct economies can be identified (Watkins 1977; Usher 1981). One economy is characterized by large capital-intensive projects, requiring imported labour, and producing significant environmental pollution. (3) The other, the traditional Aboriginal economy based, for example, on harvesting local fish and wildlife relies on local labour and small-scale technology (Sahlins 1972).

For decades the federal government has argued that the exploitation of mineral and petroleum resources is the key to launching a new approach to development in Northern Canada, beginning most stridently under Diefenbaker's "Road to Resources" program, in 1957 (Dacks 1981; Page 1986). For instance, the federal Liberal government's National

Energy Plan (NEP) proposed in 1980 supported the rapid development of oil and gas exploration in the Beaufort Sea and in the Mackenzie Delta (Brooks 1981). As a result of the NEP, many well-paying jobs on drilling rigs were created for men (particularly young men between 20 and 35) in Inuvik, Alkavik, Tuktoyuktuk, Fort Simpson and other NWT communities (McRobert 1984). This income infusion, coupled with modern transportation, enabled young Inuit men to become more mobile and gave them increased power in their communities. In some cases, contact with oil-rig co-workers from Southern Canada encouraged negative and destabilizing behavioural changes (e.g., gambling in Las Vegas, hiring of prostitutes), which contributed to marital breakdown, elevated levels of suicide, and disrupted traditional consensus decision-making processes and matrilineal power structures in Inuit and First Nation communities in the Western Arctic.

As "Trudeau's instant energy towns" such as Inuvik and Tuktoyaktuk developed, young Aboriginal women sought opportunities and joined local work forces at banks, medical facilities, and government agencies. The changes in both male and female gender roles resulted in a move away from reliance on certain country foods such as fish, smoked muskrat and even caribou. This in turn created a dependency on imported foods as many young people lost traditional trapping, fishing and hunting skills (McRobert 1983). In the past 20 years the situation has beyond much more dramatic because of the decline of sea ice conditions in Arctic communities and a massive increase in the accumulation of toxic substances in the fat of large Arctic mammals such as seals, whales and caribou and fish. As a result the ability of Aboriginal people in many communities to rely on sustainable food systems has been seriously impaired and in some communities completed undermined.

Further, the imposition of Western education systems has had several negative repercussions on traditional cultures (Hamelin 1979; Berger 1986). Prior to the 1990s, the educational materials used in Arctic and sub-Arctic schools often had implicit undercurrents that urbanism is more dignified than rural living and that mental labour is more

122

demanding than manual work. This has resulted in instabilities in Aboriginal communities, as they struggle to adjust to Western values, attitudes and habits.

C. The Introduction of Alien Socio-Technological Systems

Technology represents a concentration and distillation of both the knowledge and experience of a specific landscape over space and time.(4) Socio-technical systems have been developed and learned over decades and centuries. However, the transfer of Western-based technologies to the North has occurred over a shortened time period. Often, such accelerated knowledge transfers disrupt traditional values and techniques (Marriott 1952). Ecological relationships between human populations and certain wildlife species can be destabilized. The reduction of infant mortality (and related population growth), the development of the snowmobile, the use of modern communications equipment and planes for spotting herds of caribou, and the expansion of local markets for traditional foods have all been factors in the acceleration of local depletion of certain wildlife populations (McCandless 1985; McTaggart-Cowan 1981; Naugle 2011).

One result of the widespread and rapid adoption of exotic technology such as snowmobiles powered by gasoline (and requiring regular mechanical and electrical servicing) is the tight interconnections among new technologies, leading to overreliance on disposable products, built-in obsolescence and what some experts have termed "technological overdevelopment" (Foster 1962; Marriott 1952, 261-272).   For example, in many communities traditional technologies such as dog-powered sleds were replaced with snowmobiles (McRobert 1984; Usher 1983).   This meant that sled dog populations in communities could be reduced, a trend often encouraged by the local police and other officials to allegedly promote greater community safety (e.g., by reducing the risks associated with attacks on humans by sled dogs), and sometimes encouraged through available federal taxation and grant programs.

123

D. The Impact of Modern Communications

As McLuhan (1964) suggested, the adoption of modern space-dominating media and communications technologies also has acted to distort Aboriginal culture and social relations . Time-boundedness has been altered, and self-perception and the perception of social contexts have shifted. Oral traditions began to diminish as broadcasts of Southern Canadian and American TV programs increased (Mandlsohn 1982; Simon 2011) and Internet access expanded. For instance, the Aboriginal relationship to place, a vital part of Aboriginal cultural prior to contact with Euro-Canadians, has become less important to younger indigenous peoples while Western celebrity culture, politics, and modernization continue to assume greater importance.

An Example: Impacts of the Western ideology of "Balanced Development"

In 1972 the Department of Indian Affairs and Northern Development (DIAND; renamed the Department of Aboriginal and Northern Affairs in 2012) published Canada's North 1970-1980 (Canada, DIAND 1972) and heralded a move towards "balanced development." However, the irony of "balanced development" is that it was conceived in tandem with plans to develop oil and gas reserves in the Western Arctic and build a massive pipeline up the Mackenzie Valley to southern Canada (Rees 1982; 1983). In response to protests from Aboriginal groups in Northern Canada, religious leaders and an increasingly vocal public, the federal Liberal minority government appointed an inquiry led by Justice Tom Berger. After three years of work, the Inquiry released a report called the Northern Frontier, Northern Homeland (Canada, Report of the Mackenzie Valley Pipeline Inquiry 1977; hereinafter Berger 1977).

The Inquiry reversed the usual flow of information between Canada's economic centres and the hinterland; northern Aboriginal criticisms, concerns and aspirations, informed by their traditional values and customs were recognized as valid. In addition, the Berger Inquiry

124

highlighted that DIAND's so-called proposed balanced development policy lacked explicit provisions on exactly how environmental protection could be achieved and Aboriginal rights protected.

An excellent example of the failure of balanced development is oil and gas development in the Beaufort Sea-Mackenzie Delta Region (BSMDR) in the early 1980s. The Beaufort Sea Hydrocarbon Production Proposal (BSHPP) was said to represent an attempt to integrate conservation and development. It was proposed that the BSMDR would have dozens of drilling and production facilities, resulting in the creation of an extensive infrastructure. Essentially, the BSMDR would become a heavily industrialized region overnight (Beakhurst 1983; Tull 1983; Usher 1982).

However, the failure of "balanced development" was exemplified by the one-way information flow during the cosmetic 'consultation' process between the BSHPP proponents industry and Aboriginal and Inuvialiut communities of the Western Arctic. Unfortunately, this limited "public participation" seemed sufficient to legitimize the development in the region in the eyes of industry and the federal bureaucracy (Beakhurst 1983; McRobert 1983b).

The BSMDR cost taxpayers hundreds of millions of dollars. However, the massively subsidized discoveries were insufficient to justify the cost. In addition, drilling in the Arctic Ocean was dangerous and far more complex then initially imagined (Page 1986). After the federal election of 1984 Aboriginal and Northern communities in the BSMDR experienced a severe economic "bust." The Mulroney Progressive Conservative government shifted large federal investments and tax breaks back to conventional supplies and the oil sands in Western Canada, as well as new potential supplies in Newfoundland and Nova Scotia (Page 1986). While many Aboriginal and Inuit communities had an increased appetite for economic growth and entrepreneurship, oil and gas companies and support industries simultaneously exited the region. This left Aboriginal communities with seriously disrupted traditional economic and social frameworks, and unsupported new socio-technological systems.

Social and Ecological Impacts Evident in Northern and Arctic Communities Today

Social Impacts

As discussed above, the introduction of Western ideologies and values has seriously affected traditional Aboriginal values, behaviours and socio-economic systems. For example, statistically, the rate of violence in Nunavut is seven times the Canadian average. The homicide rate in Inuit communities is ten times the Canadian average. Inuit males aged 15-24 are 40 times more likely to commit suicide then the rest of their peers in Canada (White 2011). Child abuse in Inuit communities is ten times the national average. Seven to ten preschoolers grow up without adequate food. In 2010, Nunavut ranked last in Canada on: education, general health, employment, income and housing. The crime rate is also increasing and the average number of prisoners, waiting for court dates increased from 18 in 1999, to 63 in 2010 (White 2011). The unemployment rate for Nunavut is approximately 20 per cent, and only 7 per cent of the Territory's revenue is generated internally (White 2011). As King (2012) explains, the efforts of the Inuit to settle their land claim and promote self-government in the new territory of Nunavut in the past 15 years have not addressed many of these fundamental challenges. Unfortunately these statistics are representative of the much larger social and economic problems evident in many Northern Aboriginal communities.

Ecological and Social Impacts of Climate Change

Climate change also has exacerbated the social dislocation of northern Aboriginal communities because Arctic ice continues to be younger and thinner, and the permafrost has become increasingly unstable, making traditional hunting and fishing more difficult. In the early 1980s 40 per cent of Arctic ice was more than five years old. This declined dramatically to five per cent in 2011 (Emmerson and Lahn 2012, 13). The environmental conditions in the Arctic have impacted living ecosystems. There have been losses in walrus and polar bear populations, and warmer ocean temperatures have harmed some marine life and the fish stocks associated (Emmerson and Lahn 2012, 14). Warmer waters have also enabled fish stocks to migrate northwards, resulting in the introduction of new invasive species in the Arctic environment. For example, shorter hunting seasons, increased marine pollution, and shorter winter road seasons have reduced traditional food availability for many Inuit communities (Emmerson and Lahn 2012, 15).

Pressure to assert Sovereignty

Circumpolar nations including Canada, the U.S., Denmark, Norway and Russia are under increasing pressure to develop oil and gas and to assert sovereignty. Development interest is growing in four key sectors: mineral resources (e.g., oil, gas, and mining), fisheries, logistics (e.g., shipping), and Arctic tourism (Gerhardt et al. 2010) In 2008, the United States Geological Survey (USGS) estimated that approximately 90 billion barrels of oil and 1,670 trillion cubic feet of natural gas could be available for development in the Arctic. (USGS 2008) In the past three years, the Russians, Chinese, Indians and other nations have undertaken exploratory drilling or attempted to stake a claim to Arctic oil and gas resources or, supported by massive subsidies provided by their respective governments. (Funk 2014)

Bill C-38 and Reduction of Aboriginal Rights to Participate

Bill C-38, the Jobs, Growth and Long-term Prosperity Act, was enacted by the current Conservative federal government on June 29, 2012 and introduced a number of changes that do not bode well for improving Arctic protection and Aboriginal rights. An overview of the changes include: significant amendments to the Fisheries Act and Canadian Environmental Assessment Act; limiting environmental group and Canadian public access to approval hearings; speeding up environmental reviews, slashing Environment Canada's budget; and silencing scientists (West Coast Environmental Law Association 2012).

In general, the changes to environmental laws and regulations have offloaded responsibility from the federal government to the provinces and territories. There also has been a significant narrowing of public engagement and the availability of standing and funding to participate in resource review panel hearings, particularly for major oil projects, pipelines and mines. This means that important concerns may no longer be received at public hearings. In order to participate, interested parties and the public will have to prove they will be directly affected or have relevant information or expertise. In some cases, their contributions may still be ignored. Aboriginal peoples heavily rely on public hearings as a forum for their opinions, and now there have been significant cuts in access and funding, limiting their ability to participate in decisions that will ultimately directly impact their communities

Environmental Impacts in the Arctic: The Future

There are significant knowledge gaps regarding the Arctic and sparse data exists regarding environmental baselines (Canadian Arctic Resources Committee 2010; Fridtjof Nansens Institute 2012). For example, the number of open-water days in the Arctic has led to increased coastal erosion. Warmer ocean waters, and rising sea levels, places costal infrastructure at risk. An increase in the frequency of extreme Arctic weather (e.g., flooding, forest fires, or hotter than average summers) places both individual and communities at risk (Emmerson and Lahn 2012, 16). As documented by the PEW Charitable Trusts (PEW), development in the Arctic may also lead to the creation of significant sources of air pollution, resulting from industrial activities such as shipping, smokestacks and diesel engines (PEW 2013) which could contribute to health problems in regional communities such as asthma and heart problems.

A significant risk is also posed by persistent organic pollutants (POPs). POPs are long lasting pollutants that become more concentrated as they move up the food chain (PEW 2013). The highest level of POPs are found in top predators such as polar bears, whales and seals (PEW 2013), toxins can be passed from prey to predators, and from mothers to offspring, via pregnancy and milk (PEW 2013). As marine mammals have the highest concentration of POPs, this endangers the ability of Aboriginal communities to maintain sustainable livelihoods as it removes or significantly diminishes these traditional food sources.

Already changes in Arctic sea ice are having global impacts and have resulted in "anomalously large winter snowfall across Europe, North America, and East Asia" (Emmerson and Lahn 2012, 17). Additionally "the feedback loops that lead to [the] 'Arctic amplification' [effect]... tend to accelerate global warming, while methane release from the melting of both onshore and seabed permafrost may increase atmospheric greenhouse gas concentration" (Emmerson and Lahn 2012, 17).

The Canadian federal government, like other national governments, has also been looking with ever-increasing interest at large alternative, non-conventional sources, such as methane hydrate. A tiny fraction of methane hydrate is buried in the permafrost around the Arctic Circle (USGS 2008; Mann 2013). Supposedly this represents an additional reason for exploiting resources in the Canadian North. However, Arctic and Northern communities presently do not have the requisite technological capacity to locate and extract methane hydrate. Thus, it seems Arctic and Northern communities will experience a boom and bust cycle, furthering compromising their ability to achieve sustainability in the future and repeating patterns of social disruption associated with staples resource extraction in 18th, 19th and 20th centuries. These patterns of social disruption were graphically evidenced by the Yukon Gold Rush in the late 19th century near Dawson City and subsequent mining and oil and gas development projects undertaken in the wake of Diefenbaker's Road to Resources program in the late 1950s and through the 1960s, 1970s and under the federal Liberal government's NEP into the early 1980s.

Environmental Change and the Future of Arctic Shipping

To ensure that Arctic communities are able to achieve a degree of long term sustainability and residents can maintain sustainable livelihoods well into the 21st century, First Nations, Inuit and other northern communities must become part of decision-making processes related to resource development, tourism and socio-cultural development instead of just responding to the decisions of others. As such, it is crucial that Aboriginal stakeholders play a substantial and effective role in Arctic planning (Fridtjof Nansens Institute 2012) The future of Arctic shipping is one area that already requires significant decision-making, and in which Arctic communities should have a decisive voice. This is because Arctic shipping, as discussed below, is likely to have a huge impact on the Arctic environment and Northern communities.

The majority of scientific data suggests that the polar ice caps will dissipate by 2050 at the latest. (Vallentgoed 2012, 6). Recent observed historic lows in Arctic sea ice, together with climate model projections of additional ice reductions in the future, have fueled speculations of potential new trans-Arctic shipping routes (Johnston and Timco, 2008). Currently 90% of all international trade is conducted by shipping (Blunden 2012; Vallentgoed 2012, 7). As a result, open Arctic shipping routes will have enormous potential (Smith and Stephenson 2012). Arctic shipping has already grown by leaps and bounds. In 2012, which set a record for lowest sea ice extent, a total of 46 ships—the most ever—traversed the Arctic Ocean (Smith and Stephenson 2012). Thirty-four ships made the passage in 2011 whereas just four had done so the year before. If the polar cap rescinds completely, the most direct shipping path would cut through the centre of the Arctic Ocean (Arctic Council 2009; Blunden 2012), traversing multiple national jurisdictions.

The fragility of Arctic ecosystems makes ensuring proper waste procedures and preventing discharges or accidents a pressing regulatory challenge. Additional concerns exist regarding the significant differences between the regulatory regimes, standards and the governance capacities of Arctic states to respond to environmental disasters (Blunden 2012; Dosman, 1976; Transport Canada 1998). In addition, the environmental consequences of a single oil tanker accident in the Arctic Ocean can be severe as the "semi-enclosed geography [of the Arctic] can trap pollutants for decades" (Vallentgoed 2012, 11). The high absorption capacity of ice and snow would also act to carry pollutants long distances.

Increased shipping will also undoubtedly bring new invasive alien species to Arctic Oceans as well as to Northern ports (Cressey 2011). Ballast water, stored in the ship's hull, often carries water collected in another ocean. Ships then "discharge their ballast water at new ports, therefore introducing any potential species picked up in their port of origin and releasing them into the Arctic" (PEW 2013). This presents a serious risk to the Arctic ecosystem with its low diversity of species (PEW 2013). Without established predators, new invasive forms of life could thrive in the Arctic ecosystem, overtaking current populations (PEW 2013).

The Arctic is also susceptible to the ecological problems caused by sewage and oil waste dumping (PEW 2013; Vallentgoed 2012, 13). More frequent vessel traffic, seismic testing and other industrial activities will also lead to a significant increase in noise pollution in Arctic waters, negatively impacting marine life (PEW 2013). Although international laws, regulations, and guidelines exist, these regulatory mechanisms are considered "soft law" to the extent that they are extremely difficult to enforce in the international and domestic courts. As international organizations are only able to implement "soft law", it is clear that a strong regulatory enforceable framework must be established, which includes coordinated mandatory reporting and surveillance (Vallentgoed 2012, 41). For example, an oil spill of the magnitude of the Mexican Gulf Oil spill that occurred in 2010 would be catastrophic in the Arctic, especially as Pimlott (1976) and Livingston (1981) have suggested, if large portions of spilled oil became trapped under the ice.

Conclusion: Alternatives Ideologies and Approaches

This paper has sought to highlight some of the negative social and environmental impacts caused by the imposition of Western-based

131

ideologies about resource management, economic, legal, and socio-cultural systems on Aboriginal communities in the Canadian Arctic and sub-Arctic. Canadians, including academics, the media, politicians and lawyers have a responsibility to ensure that their work reflects the challenges evident in Canada's Arctic and Northern regions and helps to raise awareness.

In 2005 and 2006, former Liberal government leader, Paul Martin, took steps while still in office to remind Canadians of the appalling conditions facing hundreds of Aboriginal communities when he began discussions that led to the progressive but ill-fated Kelowna Accord. In the 2006 federal election campaign, the Conservative Party indicated that it would not support the Accord as written. Instead, the current Conservative federal government has rolled out a conventional, military-led and economically driven model for Arctic development implemented from economic centres in Southern Canada, the U.S. and even China. Unfortunately, this vision for the North fails to fully address the massive cultural, social, health, and environmental problems that it is bound to cause for Northerners, especially Aboriginal peoples, in the long term.

Due to factors like the serious climatic fluctuations in the North, development and ecosystem management strategies derived from research on and experience with mid-latitude ecosystems seem doomed to failure. Moreover, questionable strategies such as "balanced development" have inherent paradoxes, creating distortions and imbalances. Instead, Aboriginal communities wanting to achieve sustainability need to re-focus on import substitution (DPA Group 1986; Huskey 1984), promotion of local food supplies, community building, renewable energy development, and retaining local jobs.

An effective alternative for the management and planning of development in Northern communities is the implementation of co-management between Aboriginal communities and senior governments as a foundational principle (Armitage et al. 2007). Co-management policies such as those implemented as part of the James Bay Agreement

132

in 1976 and the Inuvialuit Committee for Original Peoples' Entitlement (COPE) agreement in 1978, as well as the more recent self-government treaties in the Yukon and Nunavut can help mitigate some of the pressures from conventional resource development (Armitage et al. 2007; Anderson and Nuttall, 2004). Co-management can succeed to the extent that it stresses greater local control (Schumacker 1973), slower development, increased value-added production to promote jobs and provides for the incorporation of community-based consensus processes. Co-management also enables the growth of opportunities like eco-tourism, cooperatives and alternative energy development.

In order to address the impacts of alien technologies and media, new systems of locally-controlled education and communication must also be properly implemented and funded in the North. For example, Mary Simon argues that the creation of an Inuit university, with graduating standards respected across Canada and grounded in the Inuit language, culture and worldview, would play a significant role in promoting Northern independence (Simon 2011) and sustainable livelihoods. It is also vital to affirm the role of art and culture; artists often have unique perspectives and can help to challenge the status quo and spread information widely. As part of maintaining or re-acquiring culture, northern Aboriginal communities need to increase local, relevant media programming and content and use of a collaborative approach to achieve mutual goals and cultural change.

Similarly, current economic development strategies rely on the increased importation of socio-technical systems to the North. However, this dependency should be viewed as problematic, rather than as a solution. The introduction of all new technologies should be carefully considered because, for the most part, they typically represent a loss of Aboriginal local control. If long-term dependency is not viewed as a potential problem these communities cannot hope to achieve long-term sustainable livelihoods.

ENDNOTES

(1) Parts of this article are based on research the author conducted for his Master's in Environmental Studies at York University in the early 1980s. The author acknowledges the assistance provided by Sharon Sam of the University of Ottawa Law School in preparing this article.

(2) As explained by Relph in his classic book, *Place and Placelessness* (1976), modern industrial communities are filled with Disney-like parks, shopping malls, big box stores and chain restaurants, shaped in part by the unceasing demands of consumers and multinational corporations (Barnett and Mueller 1974).

(3) When resources are exported to the metropolis, there is minimal value-added. Instead, secondary manufacturing takes place in Southern communities where the real "wealth" of industrialization is generated. This marginalizes the hinterland economy. One critic notes that the: "overdevelopment of one region depends on the underdevelopment of another; the overdevelopment of one class depends on the underdevelopment of subordinate ones (Clement 1977, 296).

(4) In the modern context, technology is described in the language of economic policy and as the organization of knowledge for the achievement of practical ends. As such it includes not only machines but also tools such as computer languages and contemporary analytical and mathematical techniques. Some economists and ecologists such as argue that technology allows humans to consume resources more efficiently (i.e. with less energy expenditure). As an alternative definition, in 1984 the author developed the following: "Technology is a sub-system of culture based on the application of knowledge, both theoretical and experiential, of a particular landscape which has been compressed in time and space" (McRobert 1984).

References

Anderson, D.G. and M. Nuttall (eds.). 2004. *Cultivating Arctic Landscapes: Knowing and Managing Animals in the Circumpolar North.* New York: Berghahn Books.

Arctic Council. 2009. *Arctic Marine Shipping Assessment 2009 Report.* Ottawa: Arctic Council.

Armitage, D., F. Berkes, F. and N. Doubleday (eds.). 2007. *Adaptive Co-Management: Collaboration, Learning, and Multi-Level Governance.* Vancouver: UBC Press.

Baldwin, A., Cameron, L. and Kobayashi, L. (eds.) 2011. *Rethinking the Great White North: Race, Nature, and the Historical Geographies of Whiteness in Canada.* Vancouver: UBC Press.

Barnet, R.J. and Mueller, R.C. 1974. *Global Reach: The Power of Multinational Corporations.* New York: Simon and Schuster.

Bates, M. 1956. "Man as an Agent in the Spread of Organisms." In *Man's Role in Changing the Face of the Earth*, edited by W.L. Thomas. Chicago: University of Chicago Press.

Beakhurst, G. 1983. *The Dene Perspective: Presentation to Beaufort E.A.P.* Ottawa, Ontario: Dec. 16.

Berger, T.R. 1979. "A Glance at History." *Northern Perspectives* 7(3): 1-5.

_____. 1986. *Village Journey: The Report of the Alaska Native Review Commission.* New York: Hill and Wang.

Blunden, M. 2012. Geopolitics and the Northern Sea Route. *Int Aff* 88(1):115–129, 10.1111/j.1468-2346.2012.01060.

Brody, H. 1975. *The People's Land.* Markham: Penguin Books.

------------ 1983. *Maps and Dreams: Indians and the British Columbia Frontier.* Markham: Penguin Books.

Brooks, D. 1980. "Black Gold: The Beaufort Oil Rush." *Northern Perspectives* 8(6): 1-7.

------------- 1981. Zero Energy Growth for Canada. Toronto: McClelland and Stewart.

Calef, G. 1981. *Caribou and the Barren-Lands.* Ottawa: Canadian Arctic Resources Committee/Firefly.

Canada, DIAND. 1972. *Canada's North, 1970-1980: A Policy*

Statement on Northern Development. Ottawa: Supply and Services.

Canada, Mackenzie Valley Pipeline Inquiry. *Northern Frontier, Northern Homeland: Report of the Mackenzie Valley Pipeline Inquiry.* Ottawa: Supply and Services, 1977. Commissioner: Thomas Berger.

Canada, Department of the Environment (DOE). 1982. *Canada's Special Places in the North: An Environmental Perspective for the '80's.* Ottawa: Ministry of Supply and Services.

Canada, Science Council of Canada. 1977. *Northward Looking: A Strategy and a Science Policy for Northern Development.* Ottawa: Ministry of Supply and Services.

Canadian Arctic Resources Committee. 2010. "Arctic Science". http://www.carc.org/index.php?option=com_content&view=artic le&id=160%3Aarctic-science&catid=57%3Arecommendations-for-canadian-foreign-policy&Itemid=181

Clement, W. 1977. *Continental Corporate Power: Economic Linkages Between Canada and the United States.* Toronto: McClelland and Stewart.

Colinvaux, P. 1980. *The Fates of Nations: A Biological Theory of History.* New York: Simon and Schuster.

Committee for Original Peoples' Entitlement (COPE). 2013. The Western Arctic Claim: Inuvialuit Final Agreement, as amended. Inuvik, NWT: Inuvialuit Regional Corporation. Undated. Accessed May 20, 2013. www.inuvialuitland.com/resources

Cooley, R. 1963. *Politics and conservation: the decline of the Alaska salmon.* New York: Harper and Row.

Cressey, D. 2011. "Scientific challenges in the Arctic: Open water. *Nature* 478: 174–177. Accessed November 20, 2012. doi: 10.1038/478174a.

Dacks, G. 1981. *A Choice of Futures: Politics in the Canadian North.* Agincourt, Ont: Methuen Publications.

The DPA Group Inc. 1986. *Assessment of Import Substitution Opportunities: Canada/Yukon Economic Development*

Agreement. Prepared for: Economic Policy, Planning and Research Department of Economic Development, Mines and Small Business, Yukon Territorial Government.

Dome Petroleum, Esso Resources and Gulf Canada. 1982. *Environmental Impact Statement for Hydrocarbon Development in the Beaufort Sea – Mackenzie Delta Region*. Calgary: Dome Petroleum Ltd.

Dosman, E. 1976. *The National Interest*. Toronto: McClelland and Stewart.

Elliot-Meisel, E. 2009. "Politics, pride, and precedent: The United States and Canada in the northwest passage." *Ocean Dev Int Law* 40(2):204–232.

Emmerson, C., and G. Lahn, 2012. *Arctic Opening: Opportunity and Risk in the High North*. London: Chatham House-Lloyd's Risk Insight Report.

Exxon Valdez Oil Spill Trustee Council (EVOSTC). Lingering Oil: Oil Remains: The Persistence, Toxicity, and Impact of the Exxon Valdez Oil. Accessed May 20 2013. <http://www.evostc.state.ak.us/recovery/lingeringoil.cfm>.

Fridtjof Nansens Institute. 2012. Arctic Resource Development: Risks and Responsible

Management (electronic resource). http://www.fni.no/doc&pdf/ONS-Arctic-summary.pdf.

Foster, G. 1962. *Traditional Cultures and the Impact of Technological Change*. New York: Harper and Row Publishers.

Funk, M. 2014. *Windfall: The Booming Business of Global Warming*. New York: Penguin.

Gerhardt H, PE Steinberg PE, J. Tasch, SJ Fabiano, R. Shields. 2010. "Contested sovereignty in a changing Arctic." Ann Assoc Am Geogr 100(4):992–1002.

Habermas, Jurgen. 1976. *Legitimation Crisis*. Translated by John Viertel. Boston: Beacon Press.

Hamelin, L.-E. 1979. *Canadian Nordicity: It's Your North, Too*. Trans. W. Barr. Montreal: Harvest House.

Harari, Y. 2014. *Sapiens: A Brief History of Humankind*. New York:

Signal.

Hartman, G. 1981. "Managing Non-Native Renewable Resource Use in the North: Rising Expectations in Unproductive Ecosystems." In Freeman (ed.), *Proceedings of First International Symposium on the Economy of the North*, Ottawa: ACUNS.

Hollings, C.S. (ed.), 1978. *Adaptive environmental assessment and management*. London: John Wiley & Sons.

Hollings, C.S. and Allen, Craig R. (eds.). 2008. *Discontinuities in Ecosystems and Other Complex Systems*. New York, NY: Columbia University Press.

Huskey, L. 1984. Import Substitution in Frontier Regions. Paper presented to Western Regional Science Conference, Monterey California; February 1984.

Innis, H. A. 1930. *The Fur Trade in Canada*. Toronto: University of Toronto Press.

_____. 1972. *Empire and Communications*. Toronto: University of Toronto Press.

Johnston M.E., and Timco G.W. (2008). *Understanding and Identifying Old Ice in Summer, Technical Report CHC-TR-055*, National Research Council Canada, Canadian Hydraulics Centre (Ottawa) (Transport Canada, Ottawa).

King, T. 2012. T*he Inconvenient Indian: A Curious Account of Native People in North America.* Toronto: Doubleday Canada.

Liu, M. and Kronbak J. 2010. "The potential economic viability of using the Northern Sea Route (NSR) as an alternative route between Asia and Europe." *J Transp Geogr* 18(3):434–444, 10.1016/j.jtrangeo.2009.08.004

Livingston, J. 1981. *Arctic Oil.* Toronto: CBC Publishing.

Macpherson, A. 1981. "Wildlife Conservation and Canada's North." *Arctic* 34(2): 103- 107.

Mandlsohn, Anne. 1982. "The Inukshuk Project: Communications and Technology in the Eastern Arctic." Paper presented to ES616 Communications, Technology and Social Policy, Faculty of Environmental Studies, April 1982.

Mann, Charles. 2013. "What if We Never Run Out of Oil?" *The Atlantic*,

April 24.

Marriot, McKim. 1952. "Technological Change in Overdeveloped Rural Areas." *Economic Development and Cultural Change* 1: 261-272.

Mayes, R. 1982. "Contemporary Inuit Society." *The Musk-ox* 30: 36-47.

McCallum, John. 1996. "Safe Speed in Ice: An Analysis of Transit Speed and Ice Decision Numerals." Paper prepared for Ship Safety Northern (AMIS), Transport Canada.

McCandless, R. 1985. *Yukon's Wildlife: A Social History.* Edmonton: University of Alberta Press.

McLuhan, M. 1964. *Understanding Media: The Cultural Extensions of Man.* New York: Mentor.

McRobert, D.S. 1983a. "Wildlife Management and Native Land Use in Northern Canada: A Discussion Paper." In: D. S. McRobert (ed.) *Northern Science: Fact or Fiction.* (2012) Charleston, S.C.: Createspace/Amazon.

_____. 1983b. "The Beaufort Sea EARP as an Objectivity Ritual". In: D. S. McRobert (ed.) *Northern Science: Fact or Fiction.* (2012) Charleston, S.C.: Createspace/Amazon.

_____. 1984. *The Consequences of Balanced Development in Northern Canada: The Ecological Implications of an Exotic Ideology.* Unpublished Major Paper for Master of Environmental Studies degree, Faculty of Environmental Studies, York University, Downsview, Ontario. 494 pp.

_____ (ed.). 2012. *Northern Science: Fact or Fiction.* Charleston, S.C.: Createspace/Amazon.

McTaggart-Cowan, I. 1981. *Wildlife Conservation Issues in Northern Canada.* Canadian Environmental Advisory Council, Report No. 11.

Mooney, Harold A. 2000. *Invasive Species in a Changing World.* Washington: Island Press.

Naugle, D. (ed.) 2011. *Energy Development and Wildlife Conservation in Western North America.* Washington: Island Press.

Page, R, 1986. *Northern Development: The Canadian Dilemma.* Toronto: McLelland and Stewart.

Pimlott, D.H., 1976. *Oil under the ice.* Ottawa: Canadian Arctic Resources Committee.

Portmann, A. 1961. Ani*mals as Social Beings.* Translated by Oliver Coburn. New York: The Viking Press, 1961. 1st Edition in English.

The PEW Charitable Trusts (PEW). 2013. "Pollution." Last accessed May 20 2013. oceansnorth.org/pollution.

Rees, W. 1978. *Development and planning north of 60 Degrees: Past and future.* In: R. F. Keith and J. Wright (eds.) Northern Transitions: Proceedings of the Second National Workshop On People, Resources and the Environment North of 60. Ottawa: Canadian Arctic Resources Committee.

_____. 1982. "Planning on our Arctic Frontier: Setting the Stage." Plan Canada 21(4):107-116.

Relph, 1976. *Place and Placelessness.* London: Pion.

Riddington, R. 1982. Technology, Worldview and Adaptive Strategy in a Northern Hunting Society. *Canad. Rev. Soc. and Anth.*, 19 (4).

Sahlins, M. 1972. *Stone Age Economics.* Chicago: Aidine.

Schoyen, H and Brathen, S. 2011. "The Northern Sea Route versus the Suez Canal: Cases from bulk shipping." *J Transp Geogr* 19(4):977–983, 10.1016/j.jtrangeo.2011.03.003

Schumacker, E.F. 1973. *Small is Beautiful: Economics as if People Mattered.* New York: Abacus.

Simon, Mary. 2011. "For the next generation of Inuit hope lies in education." The Globe and Mail, April 6.

Smith, Laurence and Scott R. Stephenson. 2012. "New Trans-Arctic shipping routes navigable by midcentury." Proceedings of the National Academy of Sciences of the United States of America 110. March 4, 2013 www.pnas.org/cgi/doi/10.1073/pnas.1214212110

Stabler, J.C. and Olfert, M.R. 1980. "Gaslight Follies: The Political Economy of the Western Arctic." *Canadian Public Policy* Spring 1980.

Transport Canada. 1998. The Arctic Ice Regime Shipping System; Accessed May 20, 2012.

Tull, C. Eric. 1983. The Quality of the EIS and the Need for Further

Hearings. Submission to Beaufort Sea EAP, Inuvik, November
1983. Ottawa: Beaufort Sea Alliance.

United States Geological Survey (USGS). 2008. 90 Billion Barrels of
Oil and 1,670 Trillion Cubic Feet of Natural Gas Assessed in the
Arctic. http://www.usgs.gov/newsroom, July 7, 2008.

Usher, Peter J. 1971. *The Bankslanders: Economy and Ecology of a
Frontier Trapping Community 3 Vols.* Northern Science
Research Group. NSRG – 71-2. Ottawa: DIAND.

_____. 1972. "The Use of Snowmobiles for Trapping on Banks
Island." *Arctic* 25(3): 171-181.

_____. 1981. "Staple Production and Ideology in Northern
Canada." In: W. Melody et al. (Eds.). *Culture, Communication
and Dependency.* Norwood, New Jersey: Ablax Publishing.

_____. 1982. Assessing the Impact of Industry in the Beaufort
Sea Region: A Report Prepared for the Beaufort Sea Alliance.
Ottawa: BSA.

_____. 2004. "Caribou Crisis or Administrative Crisis? Wildlife
and Aboriginal Policies on the Barren Grounds of Canada, 1947-
60." In: Anderson, David G. and Nuttall, Mark (eds.). 2004.
*Cultivating Arctic Landscapes: Knowing and Managing Animals
in the Circumpolar North.* New York: Berghahn Books.

Valaskakis, K., Sindell, P., Smith, J.G., amd Fitzpatrick-Martin,
I. 1979. *The Conserver Society: A Workable Alternative
for the Future.* New York: Colophon Book.

Vallentgoed, Darren. 2012. "Open Seas, Open Season: The impending
Challenge of Regulating the Circumpolar Shipping in the High
Arctic." Prepared for the Canadian Bar Association NEERLS'
Law School Essay Contest.

Watkins, M. 1977. From underdevelopment to development. In: M.
Watkins (Ed.) *Dene Nation: The Colony Within.* Toronto:
University of Toronto; pp. 84-102.

West Coast Environmental Law, and Ecojustice. 2012. "What Bill C-38
means for the environment." Accessed May 20 2013.
http://wcel.org/

White, P. (2011). "The Trials of Nunavut: Lament for an Arctic nation"

The Globe and Mail, April 1, 2011.

Wilson, E.O. 2012. *The Social Conquest of Earth.* Cambridge: Harvard University Press.

World Commission on Environment and Development. (1987). *Our Common Future.* London: Oxford University Press.

Zaslow, M. 1971. *The Opening of the Canadian North.* Toronto: McClelland and Stewart.